The Development Safety Update Report (DSUR): Harmonizing the Format and Content for Periodic Safety Reporting During Clinical Trials

Report of CIOMS Working Group VII

CIOMS

Geneva 2006

ISBN 92 9036 080 1

Acknowledgements

The Council for International Organizations of Medical Sciences (CIOMS) is greatly indebted to the members of CIOMS Working Group VII, on the Development Safety Update Report (DSUR): Harmonizing the Format and Content for Periodic Safety Reporting During Clinical Trials. As has become a tradition, this CIOMS Working Group had as its members senior scientists from drug regulatory authorities and pharmaceutical companies. Each member participated actively in the discussions, drafting and redrafting of texts and their review. Although some chapters and their concepts required a number of debates and revisions, the Working Group brought the project to a successful conclusion in an efficient and expeditious manner.

CIOMS especially acknowledges those members who chaired the meetings of the Working Group for their capable leadership. CIOMS gives special thanks to Ms. Linda Hostelley, the Secretary of the Group, who sensitively reflected the views and discussions in the meeting reports, distributed the draft texts and coordinated the meetings of the editorial board.

CIOMS and the Working Group are grateful to the editorial board, comprised of Arnold Gordon, Leonie Hunt, François Maignen, Hani Mickail, Valerie Simmons, and Ellis Unger, with support from Martyn Ward. CIOMS wishes to express special appreciation to Ellis Unger as Chief Editor, and Arnold Gordon as Associate Chief Editor, who prepared and ensured the quality of the final report.

Finally, CIOMS and the Working Group are grateful for important input received from several experts outside the Group. Steven Blumenthal (Merck, US) was especially helpful in preparing the initial drafts of the sample commercial sponsor's DSUR included in the report. Several people reviewed a late draft of the full report and made valuable suggestions: Dr. Barry Arnold (AstraZeneca), Dr. Brian Davis (MHRA, UK), Dr. Brian Edwards (J&J), Ms. Cindy Engle (GSK), and Dr. Alain Micaleff (Serono).

Geneva, August 2006

Juhana E. Idänpään-Heikkilä, MD, PhD
Secretary-General, CIOMS

Table of Contents

Vision

Regular and timely review, appraisal and communication of safety information are critical to risk management during the clinical development of drugs. Whereas the overall goal of a clinical development programme is to characterize the benefit-risk relationship of the product in a particular patient population, the risk to individual trial subjects is a critical consideration during product development, at a time when the effectiveness of a product is generally uncertain. By conducting an overall appraisal of safety data at regular intervals, risks can be recognised, thoughtfully assessed, and appropriately communicated to all interested stakeholders, to support the safety of clinical trial subjects. Although the regulatory authorities in the EU, US, and some other locations currently require the submission of a periodic safety report during the conduct of clinical trials, usually on an annual basis, there are substantial differences in the format, content, and timing of the different reports. Thus, the CIOMS VII Working Group is proposing an internationally harmonized document, namely, the Development Safety Update Report (DSUR), which is modelled after the Periodic Safety Update Report (PSUR) for marketed products.

The Working Group envisions that such a report would summarize the safety experience and explain any actions proposed or taken for a clinical trial, or for an entire development programme. Although the scopes of the reports would differ, the Group envisions that both commercial and non-commercial sponsors would prepare and submit DSURs. By design, these reports will enable a seamless transition for communicating safety information to relevant stakeholders, starting at the early clinical development stage and, by aligning the DSUR with the PSUR, continuing throughout the post-approval period. It will also lead to enhanced public health protection by ensuring proper focus by all sponsors and clinical investigators on ongoing safety review throughout the life-cycle of a product, while eliminating unnecessarily different, yet redundant requirements.

The CIOMS VII Working Group hopes that its proposals on the creation of a DSUR and its content and format will be endorsed and universally implemented by all stakeholders.

The CIOMS VII Working Group also envisions a further, more ambitious objective, whereby the DSUR and PSUR are integrated into a single harmonized safety report that would cover a product throughout its lifecycle. Proposals are made for future development of such a document and process.

I

Introduction and Overview

a. Rationale for the CIOMS VII Project

The periodic analysis of evolving safety information is crucial to the ongoing assessment of risk during the clinical development of an investigational drug.[1] Regular communication of such information to regulatory authorities and other stakeholders provides an information base critical for protecting the rights and welfare of subjects participating in investigational trials. This is true not only when an investigational drug is being evaluated in an ambitious clinical development programme encompassing dozens of trials, but also when a product is being investigated in a single clinical trial, by a commercial or non-commercial (e.g., academic) sponsor.

Currently, regulations in some countries or regions require the submission of a periodic report to regulatory authorities. For example, the United States (US) Food and Drug Administration (FDA) Investigational New Drug (IND) Annual Report[2] and the European Union (EU) Annual Safety Report (ASR)[3] are required on an annual basis. In its recently published report on managing safety information during clinical trials, the CIOMS VI Working Group[4] noted that there are major differences in the requirements for these reports, and recommended the development of a new, harmonized annual safety report for regulators, namely a DSUR, that would replace current reports. The details for the format, content, and timing of such a report were beyond the scope of that Group's work, but it considered that standardizing the periodicity, content, and format of a DSUR would constitute important steps forward in minimizing the discrepancies that prevail in the information now provided to different regulators, and in enhancing the efficiency of their creation by sponsors. Preparation of such a report would also serve to reassure regulators and other interested parties that safety data have been reviewed in a timely and thoughtful manner.

---

1 Throughout this book, the term "investigational drug" is used to refer to the product that is the subject of experiment, whether it is a drug, biologic or vaccine. The EU term, Investigational Medicinal Product (IMP), is not used since by definition it refers to all products included in a trial ("new" experimental product, as well as the placebo and comparator).

2 US Code of Federal Regulations 21CFR312.33: Investigational New Drug Application Annual Reports, revised April, 2004.

3 Directive 2001/20/EC of the European Parliament and of the Council of 4 April 2001 on the approximation of the laws, regulations administrative provisions of the Member States relating to the implementation of good clinical practice in the conduct of clinical trials on medicinal products for human use, Article 17 (2): Notification of serious adverse reactions, and *Detailed guidance on the collection, verification and presentation of adverse reaction reports arising from clinical trials on medicinal products for human use,* latest version of April 11, 2006 (see http://pharmacos.eudra.org/F2/pharmacos/docs/Doc2004/april/cp%20and%20guidance%20SUSARs%2023%2004%2004.pdf or http://www.emea.eu.int/).

4 *Management of Safety Information from Clinical Trials*, Report of CIOMS Working Group VI, Council for International Organizations of Medical Sciences, Geneva, 2005.

Thus, the CIOMS VII Working Group was formed to continue the work of its predecessor Group on this topic.

It is important to remind the reader that the CIOMS VII report presents proposals and recommendations that may or may not be in agreement with current local regulations and guidance from regulatory authorities. Continued adherence to prevailing requirements and guidances is essential, unless and until CIOMS VII recommendations are officially recognised and implemented.

We note that the DSUR became an official ICH topic (ICH E.2f.) in October 2006; this CIOMS report will form the basis for their development of a Guideline.

Appendix 1 provides a listing of the Working Group members and their affiliations, along with a summary of its activities over the nearly two years spent to bring this project to fruition. Key terms used in this report and their definitions are found in the Glossary (Appendix 2).

b. Background

The purpose of the drug development process is to characterize the benefit of an investigational drug, while identifying and estimating its risks, thereby enabling an overall assessment of benefit-risk. Data regarding a product's safety (and efficacy) will thus be available for ongoing regulatory review and evaluation, ultimately to allow decisions on its authorisation and approved use. In order to enable the introduction of a new medicine within a reasonable time and at an acceptable cost, the regulatory and scientific requirements must be practicable and achievable.

The overall framework of a drug development programme with regard to safety is based on a cautious and systematic approach to identification and management of risk. In order to develop a comprehensive picture of clinical safety, investigational drugs should be closely monitored during their development to ensure that benefit-risk considerations can be evaluated for the trial subjects, and placed into proper perspective on an ongoing basis. Regular, timely, comprehensive review and evaluation of safety information are critical, not only to protect the welfare of trial subjects, but also to ensure that the appropriate data are collected, especially as new safety issues are identified. Although the proposed periodic DSUR described herein is primarily intended for submission to regulatory authorities, the information it contains might be suitable for communicating to other stakeholders as well (e.g., ethics committees, individual investigators, Data and Safety Monitoring Boards [DSMBs], etc.). The extent and type of information communicated and its timing would likely depend on the intended recipient. Ultimately, some of the information included in the DSUR may be appropriate for communication to current and future trial subjects. The Working Group makes some recommendations on this issue.

Regulations and guidelines in most countries specify the requirements for sponsors, and increasingly, investigators and their institutions, whenever they conduct clinical trials. The collection, monitoring, and regulatory reporting of safety information on trial subjects feature prominently in such regulations, usually in connection with Good Clinical Practice (GCP) requirements.[5] Traditionally, most of the regulations that describe safety reporting from clinical trials focus on the expedited reporting of Individual Case Safety Reports (ICSRs), with ICH Guideline E2A[6] generally considered the standard for defining what information must be sent to various stakeholders, and when.

Regulatory requirements for periodic reporting of safety data from clinical trials prior to the approval of a drug vary widely. Some authorities (e.g., Switzerland, European Economic Area (EEA) States, and the US) require such reports, although each country or region tends to define the format, content, and timing differently. For instance, the regulatory requirements for annual safety reports for the US[7] and the EU[8] differ in content, format, and data lock point. Appendix 3 provides a comparison of the requirements for annual safety reports for the US and the EU. In addition, unlike the situation in the US, Annual Safety Reports in the EU must be sent not only to the regulatory authorities, but also to ethics committees overseeing trials in the EU. Conversely, the US FDA IND Annual Report requirements, unlike those in the EU, call for submission of information related to manufacturing processes and formulations, as well as future development plans, information that is proprietary in nature and not appropriate for disclosure to third-party stakeholders.

Considerable progress has been made in harmonizing many aspects of *post-approval* expedited and periodic safety reporting to regulators (ICH

---

[5] ICH Guideline E6, *Guideline for Good Clinical Practice,* 1 May 1996 (http://www.ich.org), is the generally accepted international standard.

[6] ICH Guideline E2A, *Clinical Safety Data Management: Definitions and Standards for Expedited Reporting,* (http://www.ich.org)

[7] See footnote 2.

[8] See footnote 3.

Guidelines E2B(M),[9] E2C,[10] E2CA[11] and E2D[12]). Another ICH Guideline, E2E,[13] describes pharmacovigilance processes and tools for making the transition from the pre-approval to the marketing environment, so as to maintain careful monitoring of known or potential risks identified during clinical development. However, much remains to be accomplished in order to eliminate unnecessary differences and inefficiencies in periodic reporting of safety information during drug development. The current situation for pre-approval periodic reporting is similar to that which prevailed for post-approval periodic safety reporting prior to the introduction of the PSUR concept, initially by CIOMS Working Group II in 1992[14] and subsequently through ICH Guideline E2C in 1996.

As a logical step, the CIOMS VI report recommended the introduction of an annual DSUR, modelled after the PSUR, a report that would summarize the safety experience for an entire development programme. Such a standardized report could be used to inform regulators (and possibly other interested parties) on the evolving safety profile of a drug. Because the content and structure of the proposed DSUR are inherently similar to those of the PSUR, the DSUR could facilitate the transition to preparing a PSUR once the product is approved for use in medical practice. In addition, it would represent an opportunity to ensure that the same terminology and definitions are applied to both reports, when appropriate.

Discussions of safety reporting during clinical development usually focus on the obligations of commercial clinical trial sponsors, such as pharmaceutical companies, engaged in new product development programmes. However, it is also important to recognise that independent investigators in various countries and regions who conduct individual studies or groups of studies are also required under regulation to prepare the same types of periodic safety reports as company sponsors. Thus, in many regions, all sponsors of clinical trials are required to submit such safety reports, whether

---

[9] ICH Guideline E2B(M), *Maintenance of the ICH Guideline on Clinical Safety Data Management: Data Elements for Transmission of Individual Case Safety Reports* (http://www.ich.org).

[10] ICH Guideline E2C, *Clinical Safety Data Management: Periodic Safety Update Reports for Marketed Drugs* (http://www.ich.org).

[11] ICH Guideline E2CA, Addendum to ICH E2C, *Clinical Safety Data Management: Periodic Safety Update Reports for Marketed Drugs* (http://www.ich.org)

[12] ICH Guideline E2D, *Post-Approval Safety Data Management: Definitions and Standards for Expedited Reporting* (http://www.ich.org).

[13] ICH Guideline E2E, *Pharmacovigilance Planning* (http://www.ich.org).

[14] *International Reporting of Periodic Drug-Safety Update Summaries*, Report of CIOMS Working Group II, Council for International Organizations for Medical Sciences, Geneva, 1992.

part of a commercially-oriented new product development programme or not. Independent investigators (as "sponsors") are typically academics, who may not be part of, or familiar with, the regulatory-pharmaceutical company milieu. Generally these investigators may not be aware of efforts such as those under CIOMS or the International Conference on Harmonization (ICH). For example, typical non-commercial sponsors are not familiar with terminology such as Development Core Safety Information (DCSI), or Company Core Safety Information (CCSI) as used in a Periodic Safety Update Report (PSUR) for marketed products, or the concepts and practices behind them. One of the challenges for regulators and the clinical trial community, therefore, is to consider how the proposals in this report can be incorporated into practice by independent investigators.

The above considerations reflect a traditional concept, namely that separate periodic reports, perhaps with disparate formats and contents, are appropriate for pre- and post-approval conditions (i.e., a DSUR and PSUR, respectively). The Group came to the realization that preparation and submission of two separate reports is not only considerably inefficient for both sponsors and regulatory reviewers, but also less than optimally informative. Nearly all members of the Working Group felt that a single integrated periodic safety reporting model, transcending the DSUR-PSUR interface, would be ideal for tracking the safety of a product throughout its lifecycle, and that such a coordinated approach would facilitate the generation of a consistent safety message to the intended recipients of both documents. However, as the Working Group developed a conceptual framework for the DSUR, it became apparent that this deceptively simple, integrated model carries with it several difficult and important practical challenges, particularly when a product is still under development in one or more countries while on the market in others.

Chapter IV of this report provides a detailed rationale for such an integrated model, and makes some concrete recommendations for moving toward that ideal concept as a separate project. The Working Group recognises the significant and complex challenges a unified safety update report would present, such as requiring changes to existing practices and requirements. Therefore, considering the pressing need to develop the DSUR model within the current regulatory framework, the focus of this publication is on a harmonized global DSUR. Unlike the post-authorisation safety report (PSUR), designing an analogous, harmonized, pre-authorisation safety report has never been attempted. Nevertheless, it is the belief of CIOMS Working Group VII that the concept of an integrated life-cycle periodic safety report described in Chapter IV deserves to be pursued as a desirable and rational goal for the future.

c. Purpose and Objectives of a DSUR

This report recommends a standard format, content, and timing for a periodic summary report for regulatory authorities that contains safety information collected during a clinical trial or a development programme.

The main objective in preparing a DSUR is to present a periodic review and analysis of safety information in order to: 1) examine whether the information reported during the review period is in accord with previous knowledge of the product's safety; 2) describe new safety issues that could have an impact on the development programme or on an individual trial; and 3) summarize the current understanding and management of known and potential risks.[15]

In addition, an attempt should be made to conduct such a safety review from the perspective of previously demonstrated or anticipated efficacy for the study population, and anticipated benefits for the target population.[16] The DSUR is not the appropriate document to evaluate or discuss comprehensively the benefit-risk relationship for the *product*. Rather, for both a development programme and for individual trials, it should reflect upon whether identified or suspected risks to the individual patients or study population (subjects already enrolled in a trial as well as those who may be entered in the future) are medically and ethically acceptable, when weighed against the presumed advantages. It would also be appropriate for the sponsor to discuss any new evidence that might have an impact on the presumed advantages, in particular if the information could alter the acceptability of

---

[15] The term "potential risk" as used here is in accord with usage in ICH Guideline E2E. It implies that there are existing data suggesting an ADR or association (but not enough evidence for a definitive decision, i.e., what might also be called a "suspected risk") as well as a risk based on theory, class effects or other factors. See the Glossary for the official definition of potential risk.

[16] Distinction is usually made between efficacy (therapeutic effect in clinical research) and benefits (effects in the "real world") (See *Benefit-Risk Balance for Marketed Drugs: Evaluating Safety Signals*, Report of CIOMS Working Group IV, Council for International Organizations of Medical Sciences, Geneva, 1998). It is important to remember that use of the expression "benefit-risk relationship" is customarily associated with products following market authorisation. In this context, determination of a medically acceptable benefit-risk relationship is a result of a regulatory decision on an application to market a product. Particularly during a development program, when treatment is blinded and confirmation of efficacy is usually not available until well into Phase II trials and beyond, it is extremely difficult if not impossible to provide a full evaluation of efficacy or benefits for a product. Even under the best of circumstances, a meaningful measure of benefits versus risks for a product requires judgement and does not lend itself to quantitative metrics.

previously identified risks. Finally, the report should consider how important risks have been managed within the development programme. Actions that have been taken or need to be taken in the future to address emerging safety issues should be discussed.

Therefore, the DSUR is intended to:

- present all pertinent, new safety-related information, both clinical and non-clinical, since the most recent report
- provide a cumulative summary of key safety findings
- relate the clinical data to patient exposure
- provide information on any marketing authorisations in different countries and any significant variations related to safety
- provide a summary of emerging and/or urgent safety issues (e.g., a major signal identified during the period)
- include a cumulative summary list of important risks that are tracked from report to report
- indicate whether the information reported for the period is in accord with previous knowledge of the product's safety profile
- provide a summary of significant changes made during the review period to the Development Core Safety Information (DCSI), safety sections of the Investigator Brochure, or other reference safety information that might be used (for example, by independent sponsor-investigators). The version in effect at the beginning of the review period is used as the reference safety information.
- on the basis of the data, indicate whether changes should be, or have been, made to clinical trial protocols, informed consent, or the investigator's brochure/DCSI to improve management of risk; the implications of such changes should be discussed.

The CIOMS VI Working Group's report strongly recommended a formal process for regular, periodic review of aggregate safety data throughout a clinical trial programme. It is that process that should enable the detection of safety signals and allow the sponsor to place risk in perspective to the demonstrated or anticipated efficacy. The preparation of the DSUR, on the other hand, creates an opportunity for a broad, overall safety re-evaluation on an annual basis. Together with other regular and periodic safety monitoring procedures, preparation of the DSUR provides yet another opportunity to ensure that the risks to trial participants are recognised, assessed, and communicated.

It is also worth noting that the European Commission has issued a guideline on what should be considered a "potential serious risk to human health," and how it might affect the benefit-risk balance when a product reaches the market: "a situation where there is a significant probability that a serious hazard resulting from a human medicinal product in the context of its proposed use will affect public health."[17]

In addition to relevant clinical safety information, the DSUR would also contain important findings related to non-clinical research, manufacturing issues (especially important for biotechnology products), patient compliance,[18] and possibly relevant data on similar products (in the same class, for example). It would also include adverse safety findings related to protocol procedures. Much of the data included in the DSUR is intended to be interval in nature (new since the prior report), but, as discussed in detail later, some of the information, depending on its nature, should be presented cumulatively. For example, the Working Group proposes cumulative summary tabulations for serious adverse events.

One of the more controversial issues the Working Group debated was the importance of line listings of individual adverse event or adverse reaction cases in a periodic report. The majority of the Group believes that they provide limited value, and, if included in a DSUR at all, should be restricted to Suspected Unexpected Serious Adverse Reactions (SUSARs).[19] The Group believes that summary tabulations can be structured to illustrate adequately listed and unlisted serious adverse reactions.[20] Specific recommendations are provided in Chapter II, Section b.3.

Similarly, although the DSUR is intended to be a stand-alone document, there may be other types of reports with potential overlap. In addition

---

[17] Guideline on the definition of a potential serious risk to public health in the context of Article 29(1) and (2) of Directive 2001/81/EC - March 2006. See http://ec.europa.eu/enterprise/pharmaceuticals/pharmacos/new.htm or Official Journal of the European Union C133, 8 June 2006, Volume 49, Pages 5-7: http://eur-lex.europa.eu/LexUriServ/site/en/oj/2006/c_133/c_13320060608en00050007.pdf. The annex to the Guideline can be found in Notice to Applicants Volume 2C (http://ec.europa.eu/enterprise/pharmaceuticals/eudralex/vol-2/c/ser_risk_annex_h.pdf).

[18] An unusual lack of cooperation by patients in taking their medication or in adhering to other protocol requirements (e.g., self-measurements, visit schedules) might indicate an otherwise undetected safety or tolerability problem.

[19] Terminology from EU regulations; see the Glossary for details.

[20] There was also a consensus that voluminous collections of line listings included in PSURs were of even less value. More detailed discussion and recommendations on line listings are presented in Chapter III, Section j.3.

to possible duplication of information within DSURs and PSURs, sponsors may generate Development Risk Management Plans during clinical development programmes that change over time (DRMPs, as recommended in the CIOMS VI report); they may also prepare periodic updates specifically for investigators and their ethics committees. Furthermore, if the product is on the market in one or more locations, there could be potential differences between the DCSI and the CCSI, as well as differences between the CCSI and local, official data sheets. All of these possible overlaps should be considered and rationalized, particularly by commercial sponsors. Some recommendations are made in this report.

The DSUR can also provide an opportunity to facilitate other processes and obligations. For example, sponsors may wish to link the preparation of the DSUR to an annual update of the DCSI or safety sections of the Investigators Brochure. Similarly, the overall evaluation and conclusions contained within late-stage DSURs can be directly linked to a risk management plan that might be needed at the time of marketing authorisation submission or approval.

The DSUR is *not* meant to serve as any of the following:

- a formal benefit-risk assessment for the product
- a comprehensive integrated safety summary of the type used in marketing application submissions
- a repository or detailed discussion of all individual case safety reports
- a signal detection tool
- an "expert report."

This CIOMS Working Group report addresses only the responsibilities of clinical trial sponsors for periodic safety reporting. It does not discuss the process by which regulatory authorities might review and respond to such reports. However, in the interest of harmonization, the Working Group hopes that regulatory authorities can embrace the format and content of a DSUR, and urges regulators to refrain from requesting additional data, different data presentations, or other material, beyond what is specified in the DSUR, unless there is a compelling need based on a specific safety issue.

Chapters II and III, respectively, present the general principles behind the preparation and use of the DSUR, and a model DSUR. The model is illustrated with sample, fictitious DSURs for a commercial and non-commercial (trial-specific) sponsor (See Appendix 4).

II

General Principles for a DSUR

a. Administrative Matters

(1) Scope of a DSUR

The DSUR is an annual summary of safety information for an investigational drug. The scope of the report can be as narrow as a single clinical trial, or as broad as an entire clinical development programme. It is to be prepared by the sponsor of the trial(s), and is intended to afford the sponsor an opportunity to review, assess, and update the safety profile of an investigational drug, and to communicate this assessment to relevant stakeholders.

Generally, the emphasis of the DSUR will be on interventional Phase I to Phase IV clinical trials, as well as compassionate use and special access programmes during development. Other findings that impact the safety and welfare of clinical trial subjects should be included as well (see below).

For the purposes of the DSUR, interventional clinical trials are prospective studies that fulfil one or more of the following criteria:

- patients are randomised (or openly assigned) in advance to a particular therapy (blinded or open-label)
- there are defined inclusion and exclusion criteria
- monitoring or diagnostic procedures over and above normal clinical practice are included in the protocol.

Such studies are generally designed to do one or more of the following:

- characterise or verify pharmacological effects
- evaluate safety
- assess drug absorption, distribution, metabolism, and excretion.

When available and applicable, the DSUR should also contain:

- significant safety findings from non-clinical studies (including toxicological and *in vitro* studies)
- safety findings from clinical trials conducted by a co-development partner in a licensing agreement, if permitted by the contractual arrangement
- relevant safety findings from non-interventional (observational or epidemiological) studies, if conducted to characterise the natural

history of the disease area under investigation (e.g., an observational study of lymphoma associated with rheumatoid arthritis)

- any other data that may have an impact on the safety and well-being of the human subjects participating in the trials, such as: manufacturing or microbial changes (biologics), and studies recently published in the literature that bear importantly on the safety (or occasionally efficacy) of the product, or comparator, if appropriate
- a discussion of results obtained from interventional clinical trials when negative efficacy results have a direct impact on subject safety (e.g., worsening of the underlying condition if the indication is serious or life-threatening)
- information from any source on relevant findings for products in the same pharmacological or therapeutic class.

Given that clinical development of a drug often continues following marketing authorization (e.g., clinical trials may be ongoing in other countries or regions where approval has not been granted, and may be conducted in unapproved indications, formulations, or special patient populations), there are situations where findings from post-marketing studies may be relevant to ongoing interventional trials. Such findings (e.g., from observational studies, registries) should be presented in the DSUR.

(2) Information Out of Scope

Non-Interventional Studies: Routine results from non-interventional studies (e.g., observational and epidemiological studies) that are conducted for the purpose of investigating the safety of a product under approved conditions of use are generally not within the scope of the DSUR, except when the findings are relevant to subjects in ongoing clinical trials (see Chapter II.a.1., above). When such studies are relevant, only summary findings should be included in the DSUR. Details on individual serious adverse event cases from observational or epidemiological studies should generally not be included in the DSUR.

Compliance with GCP: A DSUR is not intended to address issues related to GCP compliance or discuss findings from GCP inspections.

Pharmacoeconomic Studies and Medical Practice Guidelines: Pharmacoeconomic evaluations and good medical practice guidances published by institutions such as the National Institute for Clinical Excellence (NICE) in the UK are outside the scope of the DSUR. Economic analyses and cost-benefit assessments do not inform the benefit-risk assessment during drug development, and are not within the scope of the DSUR.

Routine Efficacy Data: The DSUR is not meant to report routine clinical efficacy results.

(3) When is a DSUR Required?

The CIOMS VII Working Group recommends adoption of the DSUR as the common global standard for periodic reporting of safety data from clinical trials, thus replacing existing formats such as the US FDA IND Annual Report and the EU Annual Safety Report. The goal is to produce a harmonized and consistent perspective on the safety of an investigational drug, to be provided to regulatory authorities worldwide, who require or request a report. DSURs should be submitted throughout the lifecycle of the investigational drug, for as long as a sponsor conducts interventional clinical trials. It is possible that regulators in countries where Phase I-III clinical trials are no longer being conducted, but where the drug is marketed, may not wish to receive a DSUR.

When only Phase IV studies are conducted, a DSUR may not be necessary (see (3)iii, below).

i. Clinical Development Prior to First Approval

When an investigational drug is exclusively under clinical development (i.e., without marketing approval in any country), the DSUR provides an annual assessment of its emerging safety profile, based on data from interventional clinical and non-clinical studies undertaken by a sponsor.

ii. Clinical Development After First Approval

Clinical development of a product often continues after initial marketing authorisation (e.g., continuation of clinical development in countries or regions where approval has not yet been granted; new dosage strengths or formulations; new or related indications; evaluation in special populations). The Working Group envisions that DSURs will continue to be prepared annually after the first marketing approval of a drug, for as long as a sponsor undertakes interventional clinical studies in non-approved indications, populations, and formulations.

iii. End of Clinical Development

When a sponsor decides to terminate permanently a clinical development programme or trial, or all interventional studies have been completed for an investigational drug, the CIOMS VII Working Group recommends preparation and submission of a final ("close-out") DSUR, as soon as practicable, but ideally no later than 60 days after the latest DSUR data lock point. The purpose of this final DSUR is to ensure that outstanding safety issues have been discussed and addressed, particularly if there are implications for the safety of a product that may be marketed.

It is also possible that a commercial sponsor might decide to discontinue trials temporarily but wish to keep open the possibility of restarting a development programme at a later time.[1] Under such circumstances, it would be reasonable for sponsors to inform the appropriate regulatory authorities of such a decision.

Phase IV studies are ordinarily interventional, and their results would be included in DSURs as long as DSURs are prepared. However, under conditions when a sponsor no longer conducts any Phase I-III studies, and the only studies are Phase IV trials, it is recommended that the relevant results be presented in PSURs and that no DSUR be required.

(4) Who is Responsible for Preparing a DSUR?

Whether representing a commercial or non-commercial organization, the sponsor(s) of an investigational interventional clinical trial(s) is responsible for the preparation, content, and submission of a DSUR.

i. Commercial Sponsors

Commercial sponsors, typically pharmaceutical, biotech, device, and diagnostic product companies, are usually responsible for entire clinical development programmes. They have the infrastructure, databases, and other resources available to ensure that the DSUR for any given investigational drug is prepared and submitted to the extent and scope proposed by the CIOMS VII Working Group in this report. It is also becoming increasingly common for individual

[1] For example, in the U.S., commercial sponsors may keep an IND open even if their trial programme were halted temporarily. (In the US, sponsors are still required to submit an IND annual status report, even if only to indicate that no activity had taken place within the previous year.)

clinical studies in a development programme to involve collaboration with external contract research organizations (CROs), public and private institutions, other collaborative groups, or co-development partners. In such arrangements, whether they involve the management of a clinical trial or the preparation of a DSUR, the ultimate accountability rests with the trial sponsor, even though individual sponsor activities may have been delegated. Therefore, it is critical to ensure that, as with other outsourcing activities, an unambiguous contractual agreement has been made, detailing the respective responsibilities of the partners.

ii. Non-Commercial Sponsors

For the purpose of this report, the CIOMS VII Working Group considers a non-commercial sponsor to be an individual or organization, who is neither the manufacturer nor the patent-holder for the investigational drug.[2] Such sponsors are not usually directly supported by the manufacturer of an investigational or approved product.[3] Non-commercial sponsors can include individual academic investigators, universities, collaborative groups, and other research institutes, who sponsor clinical trial(s) under their own IND or Clinical Trial Application (CTA). Non-commercial sponsors conduct interventional clinical trials, and thereby assume the responsibilities of a sponsor, including ownership of data and preparation and submission of a DSUR.

A number of sections of the DSUR are not applicable for non-commercial sponsors. In particular, non-commercial sponsors are unlikely to submit information on manufacturing issues, non-clinical data, and marketing status. As a result, the non-commercial

---

[2] The distinction between commercial and non-commercial sponsors is not always clear. As used here, the meaning is generally the same as industry versus non-industry. Generally, "commercial" sponsors are for-profit businesses engaged in the discovery, development, manufacture, and sale of new products or new uses of already marketed products. Non-commercial sponsors are typically individual practicing physicians (or a group of physicians), either working independently or in association with a university, institute, or other organization, who conduct studies without the collaboration or participation of a commercial sponsor. However, it is possible that a university or other institution can discover and obtain a patent on a new product, on which it might conduct early clinical studies, with plans to license or sell the product to a pharmaceutical or biotech company for full development and marketing.

[3] In the EU, a manufacturer is allowed to provide direct support to a non-commercial investigator as long as the trial is not part of a development programme for a marketing authorisation; at the end of the trial, the data belong to the non-commercial sponsor, who would be responsible for preparing an Annual Safety Report under current regulations.

DSUR will tend to be abbreviated. An example of a non-commercial sponsor's DSUR is included in Appendix 4.

In some circumstances, a pharmaceutical manufacturer (commercial sponsor) will provide financial or other material support to a non-commercial sponsor and, therefore, may assume responsibility for compiling and submitting a DSUR for the investigational drug encompassing data from both sources. If, however, a non-commercial sponsor's development or interventional study(ies) are completely independent, then the non-commercial sponsor is expected to assume full responsibility for preparation of a separate DSUR.

Although CIOMS VII endorses the principle of one DSUR covering all interventional studies being undertaken by all sponsors, this is unlikely to be feasible for multiple and independent non-commercial sponsors. For example, institutional clinical trials sponsored by universities, hospitals, research centres, or academia may focus on improving the treatment or management of diseases with existing therapies (including authorised medicines, surgery, etc.). Therefore, it is likely that institutional sponsors will conduct a single trial focusing on a specific condition that involves the use of an authorised product in an unapproved indication. In these circumstances, a trial-specific DSUR by the non-commercial sponsor is appropriate.

In circumstances where multiple non-commercial sponsors (individuals, organizations, or both) are involved in a programme of clinical trials (e.g., a series of oncology studies), the Working Group recommends that if there is a principal investigator, he or she take responsibility for the preparation and content of the DSUR.

Commercial sponsors may be aware of interventional studies being conducted on their marketed products by non-commercial sponsors, either because the company has provided some support for the studies (treatment supplies, financing, technical assistance), or in the absence of such direct involvement, through other means. Typically, non-commercial sponsors will conduct Phase IV studies or possibly Phase II or III studies on unapproved uses. Under such circumstances and whenever possible, the commercial sponsor should try to obtain a copy of, at a minimum, the Executive Summary of the non-commercial sponsor's DSUR. Any relevant information would then be available for inclusion in the commercial sponsor's DSUR. If the commercial sponsor believes that the Executive Summary contains important findings, it should attempt to obtain necessary details from the investigator.

iii. Multiple Sponsors

When a sponsor is in a formal co-development or licensing relationship with one or more partners, and more than one partner is a sponsor of a clinical trial(s) with the same investigational drug, then whenever possible all of the safety information should be integrated into a single DSUR. This approach is consistent with and extends the principle of the PSUR, namely, that only one report should be submitted by all the Marketing Authorisation Holders when a drug is co-marketed by different companies. This would include situations where different doses, routes of administration, or formulations are being investigated.

Wherever possible, pharmacovigilance agreements between co-development or licensing partners should specify the exchange of safety data to ensure that a single DSUR containing all pertinent clinical trial and relevant post-marketing information can be produced by one sponsor on behalf of the alliance. This would enable each sponsor to submit the same, common document for the investigational drug, and meet their respective regulatory responsibilities, without producing separate and potentially inconsistent DSURs. Under current regulatory conditions, such arrangements may be in place for preparation of the US IND Annual Report and the EU Annual Safety Report. For this situation, and if the DSUR becomes the standard, licensing partners should ensure that their contractual agreements specify the necessary processes and procedures to accomplish this objective.

Furthermore, CIOMS VII recommends that appropriate experts from all partners in the alliance be represented in a multidisciplinary safety management team, so that the DSUR faithfully reflects the assessment and conclusions from all partners.

The submission of separate and disparate DSURs by different sponsors in a formal agreement for the same investigational drug should be the exception. When this is necessary or unavoidable, the reasons should be stated in the respective DSURs. Such reasons may include:

- When two or more sponsors have independent development programmes for different formulations or indications using the same investigational compound, there may be competitive reasons that preclude exchange of information on the overall clinical development plan at the level of detail required by a DSUR.

- The confidentiality necessary for establishing intellectual property rights may limit the ability of licensing partners to disclose seminal work in new indications using the compound, when that work is not covered by the contract.

- There are situations when significant manufacturing information, with the potential to impact safety, may be disclosed in a DSUR. Such information may need to be kept confidential.

For these reasons, it will not always be possible for licensing partners to share their respective comprehensive status reports on ongoing trials in clinical development; the data available to an individual sponsor producing a DSUR may sometimes be restricted to their own clinical development programme.

Even when two or more co-development partners prepare separate DSURs, the CIOMS VII Working Group recommends that, at a minimum, the following practices are followed:

- Individual serious adverse event reports from each partner's respective development programme should be exchanged in a timely fashion, with timelines stipulated in the safety agreement. This is necessary to ensure that appropriate safety reports (particularly those that qualify for expedited reporting by the partner) can be produced and communicated worldwide to regulators and other relevant parties.

- New non-clinical findings that represent previously unrecognised and potentially significant new safety issues for human subjects exposed to the investigational drug under development should be shared by all licensing partners.

- The licensing contract or safety data exchange agreement between the licensing partners should include provisions for sharing information related to the DSUR to the extent possible, given the above restraints.

- When separate DSURs are submitted by different partners, this should be recognised explicitly in the text of the DSURs, along with the reasons why the sponsors are unable to submit a single DSUR.
- If one of the licensing partners takes significant action(s) for safety reasons, or if there are significant actions by a regulatory authority, this information should be included in each party's DSUR.

Although the CIOMS VII Working Group acknowledges that there will be exceptions to compiling one DSUR for all development programmes using a single active drug substance, the general principle endorsed by the Working Group is to submit a single DSUR whenever possible.

(5) Recipients of the DSUR

The CIOMS VII Working Group considers that the DSUR is intended for submission exclusively to regulatory authorities. However, where national legislation requires periodic submission of safety information on an investigational drug to Ethics Committees, Institutional Review Boards, or investigators, the CIOMS VII Working Group recommends that only the DSUR Executive Summary be provided. A full DSUR could be made available upon request, but in order to protect proprietary information (such as changes in manufacturing processes), certain sections of that report may need to be redacted.

This position is based on the following considerations:

- Investigators and Ethics Committees should be kept abreast of important safety information on a regular basis, as recommended in the CIOMS VI report. Therefore, the Working Group believes that an Executive Summary of the DSUR will be sufficient to keep them informed on a broader basis.
- A DSUR may contain unblinded data, which has the potential to unblind investigators at individual study sites.
- New safety findings that could have an impact on the conduct of a clinical trial are communicated to Ethics Committees and/or investigators through other existing routes (i.e., expedited reporting, Dear Investigator letters, changes to the Investigator Brochure, and changes to Informed Consent information).

When national legislation or guidances require submission of line listings of safety case reports to Ethics Committees and/or Institutional Review Boards on a periodic basis (e.g., in the EU), the Working Group recommends that the periodicity of these line listings be coordinated with that of the DSUR so that the DSUR Executive Summary can be submitted on an annual basis with the submission of the corresponding line listing to the Ethics Committees and/or Institutional Review Boards. If national legislation precludes this alignment, then the Executive Summary should be submitted together with the first line listing following completion of the DSUR.

(6) Development International Birth Date (DIBD)

The DSUR is a periodic report, to be submitted on an annual basis. Prior to the first marketing authorisation of an investigational drug, the CIOMS VII Working Group recommends that the data lock point of the DSUR be based on the date of the first approval or authorisation to conduct an interventional clinical trial in any country. This date is termed the "Development International Birth Date" (DIBD), and is analogous to the International Birth Date (IBD) for a PSUR, defined as the date of first marketing authorisation.

However, once a product is approved in any country, the CIOMS VII Working Group recommends that the DIBD be changed to coincide with the IBD, to facilitate simultaneous preparation and alignment of the DSUR with the PSUR, and simultaneous submission of the two documents to those regulators requiring both. Adoption of a single data lock point for both reports would improve efficiency for the commercial sponsor who must prepare both reports, and synchronise analyses of the safety of the product. In addition, establishing a single data lock point for both the DSUR and PSUR supports the Working Group's vision for the eventual development and implementation of a single, integrated life-cycle safety report that incorporates the scope of the current DSUR and PSUR, and avoids duplication of information, unnecessary burden, and confusion for both sponsors and regulators (see Chapter IV).

In reaching this birth date recommendation, the CIOMS VII Working Group carefully considered both the IBD and the DIBD as options for defining the data lock point for an approved product. The Group concluded that the data lock point should be driven by the IBD, because it is already defined in ICH and national regulations, and is well understood by commercial sponsors and regulators.

The transition of the DIBD to the IBD does present some complexities regarding the periodicity for the first DSUR following initial marketing authorization. For example, assume the DIBD (and therefore the DSUR data lock point) is January 1, and the first approval occurs on April 1; the data lock point for the next DSUR under this proposal would be April 1 of the following year, and the DSUR data would therefore cover a 15-month period instead of the usual 12 months (January 1 through April 1 of the following year).[4] Toward the other extreme, if first approval occurred on October 1, in theory the next DSUR would cover 21 months (January 1 through October 1 of the following year). This represents what most would regard as an unacceptable gap in safety update reporting for a development programme, even though it would only occur for a single DSUR following initial marketing approval (subsequent DSURs would be submitted on an annual basis, using the IBD). Therefore, the Working Group recommends an approach with two possible courses of action, depending on the relation between the anniversary of the DSUR and the IBD. The goal of the plan is to permit a maximum interval of 18 months between successive DSURs in the peri-approval period.

- If initial approval occurs no more than six months after the DIBD anniversary, then the data lock point for the DSUR would become the IBD. Again, using the above example, for a drug with a January 1 DIBD and a May 1 approval, the data lock point for the DSUR would change to May 1, and the first DSUR after approval would cover 16 months.
- If the initial approval occurs more than six months after the anniversary of the IBD (e.g., August 15th approval for the above example), the Working Group recommends that the DIBD be retained as the data lock point for the first DSUR after approval (January 1; covering 12 months), but that the following DSUR would use August 15 as the data lock point (the latter report would cover only 7.5 months).

Although an arbitrary formulation, this approach would afford a convenient means to bring the DIBD and IBD into synchronisation, while providing regulators with periodic safety information covering a reasonable period of time.

---

[4] Independent of the DSUR birthday shift, it should be remembered that under common regulatory requirements, the first PSUR would still have to be prepared based on data using a data lock point that is six months from the IBD.

Exceptions can be made for non-commercial sponsors conducting a single trial of an investigational drug prior to, or following, approval. For such sponsors, their DIBD is the initial date of authorisation of their first trial in any country. The Working Group recommends use of this DIBD as the data lock point for the non-commercial sponsor's DSUR, rather than the commercial sponsor's DIBD (which would probably be unknown to the non-commercial sponsor). This practice would also be applicable for non-commercial sponsors of studies of approved drugs for new or expanded indications. For non-commercial sponsors overseeing more than one trial, the concept of one drug, one DSUR applies (see (8), below). Thus, the sponsor should develop a single DSUR, integrating data across their interventional clinical trials.

(7) Periodicity of Reporting

The DSUR should be produced on an annual basis and submitted no later than 60 calendar days from the data lock point. The assigned data lock point is either the DIBD or IBD, depending on whether or not the drug is approved in any country, as described in Section (6).

(8) A Single DSUR for an Investigational Drug

In principle, the DSUR should contain safety data arising from all interventional clinical trials conducted with the same investigational drug by a particular sponsor. Therefore, the CIOMS VII Working Group adopts the principle of the PSUR and recommends a single DSUR that incorporates the safety data from all interventional clinical trials in all indications, all dosage forms, and intended populations in which the investigational drug is being developed.

If the investigational drug is undergoing development by more than one sponsor, particularly in a co-development or other contractual agreement, the Working Group recommends that one sponsor prepare a single DSUR on behalf of the alliance wherever possible, in order to promote presentation of the complete safety profile of the investigational drug and avoid potential dilution of safety signals. Preparation of the DSUR when multiple sponsors are involved is addressed in further detail in Section (4)iii, above.

(9) Combination Therapy

The CIOMS VII Working Group recognises the potential complexities of drug development utilising combination therapies where multiple situations can prevail. As such, it is not possible to provide a single recommendation that addresses all scenarios. The Working Group has tried to consider the more commonly encountered situations below.

i. Drug-Drug Combinations

The underlying rationale for the development of drug-drug combinations is to take advantage of the individual drugs' interaction(s) to enhance efficacy, safety, or both. As such, the potential benefits and safety profile of a drug-drug combination may differ importantly from those of the individual drugs.

Examples of drug-drug combinations include regimens where two investigational drugs are administered concomitantly or sequentially by oral or parenteral routes, in fixed or variable regimens, or a new formulation containing two or more active drugs combined in a single presentation. A typical "add-on" study (where the investigational drug or comparator is added to "standard care") does not constitute a drug-drug combination.

In general, the Working Group recommends that safety information for an investigational trial or programme for a multi-drug regimen be reported in a specific DSUR for the combination (e.g., where a sponsor has only conducted studies with the combination). However, alternatively, the information specific to the combination may be incorporated into separate section(s) of one of the DSURs of the individual components of the combination as long as one of the individual drugs is under development as well. In many cases, one or more of the drugs may have prior marketing authorisation. The sponsor should select the most appropriate option based on judgement, taking into account the patient population, indication, formulation, etc., as well as the circumstances in which the trials are being conducted. The basis for this decision should be clearly explained in the report, and pertinent DSURs (as well as PSURs, if relevant) should be cross-referenced, wherever appropriate and feasible.

ii. Drug-Other Combinations

These include combinations of an investigational drug with a device, or an investigational drug combined with a biological product (cell or gene).[5] The intrinsic safety profile of an investigational drug, used in combination with a non-drug delivery system, may be modified positively or negatively, and may introduce new combination-specific safety issues. There are situations where one or more components of the combination may have gained prior approval (e.g., intranasal delivery of insulin or drug eluting stents). Alternatively, the drug and device (cell or gene) may be developed in parallel, by a single sponsor or multiple sponsors. There are situations where preparation of a combination-specific DSUR may be warranted, such as when an investigational drug and delivery device are co-developed. However, the Working Group recognises the complexities inherent in combinations of two, or potentially more drugs, devices, and biological entities, both approved and unapproved. In such situations, it may be more appropriate to present the relevant safety information for the drug-device (or biologic) combination in a separate section of the drug's DSUR. The sponsor should exercise good judgment, explain the rationale in the DSUR, and ensure proper cross-referencing when more than one DSUR is involved.

(10) Reference Safety Information

Analogous to the PSUR, an objective of the DSUR is to determine whether information recorded during the reporting period is in accord with the previous knowledge of the safety of the investigational drug, and to indicate whether changes should be made to the clinical trial(s), Investigator's Brochure, or Informed Consent, as appropriate. A single Reference Safety Information document is needed to perform this comparison. A single source provides a practical, efficient, and consistent approach to the safety evaluation, allowing the DSUR to be used as a global report accepted in all regions.

Prior to approval of the investigational drug in any country, the Working Group recommends that the safety section of the Investigators Brochure or the Development Core Safety Information (DCSI) serve as the reference safety information for the DSUR. If the product is subsequently approved, the DCSI should be aligned and harmonized

[5] In the EU, most cell-derived products and administered genes are considered to be medicinal products; therefore, they would not be referred to as "non-drugs" in that region.

with the Company Core Safety Information (CCSI),[6] as appropriate. When doing so, consideration must be given to possible differences in safety profiles that arise from different indications, formulations and populations that might be under study or development.

The Working Group also recommends that any differences between the product information used as a reference in the DSUR and local product information/labelling where the product is marketed be noted in the covering letter accompanying the local submission of the DSUR, when applicable.

Non-commercial sponsors who have to prepare DSURs may not have access to the safety reference information documents mentioned above, especially the CCSI. Therefore, they should clearly state the reference information that has been used (e.g., for approved products, it is expected that the local product information/labelling would be used).

(11) Relationship of DSUR to Other Documents

It is important that when sponsors prepare a DSUR they understand its possible relationship to other documents and reports covering pharmacovigilance.

i. PSUR

Once a product is approved, the sponsor who is also the marketing authorisation holder is responsible for the preparation of a PSUR in addition to the continued preparation of DSURs for as long as the product is being investigated in unapproved indications, patient populations, or formulations. Therefore, the CIOMS VII Working Group recommends inclusion of relevant PSUR summary information in the DSUR (e.g., post-approval patient exposure data, key safety findings from spontaneous cases and observational studies; see Chapter III.n.). It is also recommended that the PSUR executive summary be included with the DSUR.

This proposal will only apply for as long as separate DSUR and PSUR documents are required. Refer to Chapter IV for the vision of the CIOMS VII Working Group to achieve an integrated periodic safety update report throughout the entire product lifecycle.

---

6 For discussion of the DCSI and CCSI and their relationship, see *Management of Safety Information from Clinical Trials,* Report of CIOMS Working Group VI, Council for International Organizations of Medical Sciences, Geneva, 2005

ii. Development Risk Management Plan (DRMP)

In accordance with a recommendation from the CIOMS VI Working group, and consistent with recently published FDA Risk Management Guidance documents[7] and ICH Guideline E2E, the Working Group suggests that the DRMP should be aligned with the DSUR. DSUR preparation and review, and update of the DRMP should be performed in such a way as to maintain consistency of the information contained in the two documents.

iii. Periodic SUSAR Line Listings

In accordance with recommendations from the CIOMS VI Working Group, as well as some local/regional requirements (e.g., in the EU), periodic SUSAR Line Listings can be sent to Investigators and Ethics Committees in place of individual case report safety mailings. CIOMS VII proposes that the Executive Summary of the DSUR be appended or included with the next scheduled line listing after completion of the DSUR (See also Section (5), above).

(12) Confidentiality

Given the scope and proposed content of a DSUR, these reports will contain confidential information. There are two main confidentiality issues: the identities of study subjects and proprietary information. This issue is also discussed in the ICH Guideline E2C addendum on PSURs, which recognises the confidentiality of the data and conclusions reached in a PSUR. Similar considerations apply to the DSUR:

- The data elements in the adverse drug reaction reports included in a DSUR may contain some personal information on the subjects enrolled in a clinical trial. In particular, there may be some instances where the information on a subject enrolled in the clinical trial may allow the identification of an individual patient (e.g., for products aimed at treating rare diseases).
- The DSUR may contain proprietary and commercially confidential information on the development of an investigational drug. For in-

[7] *FDA Guidance for Industry: Premarketing Risk Assessment, Development and Use of Risk Minimization Action Plans, Good Pharmacovigilance Practices and Pharmacoepidemiologic Assessment*, March 2005 (http://www.fda.gov/cder/guidance/6357fnl.htm, http://www.fda.gov/cder/guidance/6358fnl.htm, and http://www.fda.gov/cder/guidance/6359OCC.htm).

stance, the simple disclosure of the existence of a study, its protocol title, and targeted sample size, are all potentially sensitive for competitive reasons.[8] Companies have legitimate business reasons for wanting to keep such information out of the public domain. Other considerations include the impact of public disclosure of a DSUR when it contains findings from a completed study planned for submission to a journal for publication. If the results are made available under local "Freedom of Information" provisions, such disclosure may negatively impact the acceptability of study data for publication.

Confidentiality of this information must be balanced with the obligations of regulatory authorities around the world to make appropriate clinical safety and pharmacovigilance information publicly available. In this regard, the information contained in the DSUR should be treated in accordance with the provisions of the World Medical Association Declaration of Helsinki,[9] the ICH Guideline for Good Clinical Practice (ICH E6), and the applicable national data protection acts which address personal, proprietary, and commercially confidential information.

Similar to the recommendations made in the addendum to ICH Guideline E2C, the CIOMS VII Working Group recommends that the title page of the DSUR contain a statement on the confidentiality of the data and conclusions included in the report. (See also Chapter III.a. and Appendix 4.)

b. Technical Content

(1) Sources of Data

i. Interventional Clinical Trials

The DSUR should cover all interventional studies that are ongoing or completed during the review period including:

- clinical trials conducted during the development of an investigational drug (Phase I – III trials)

---

8 "*Joint Position on the Disclosure of Sensitive Information via Clinical Trial Registries and Data Bases*," International Federation of Pharmaceutical Manufacturers and Associations (IFPMA), September 2005. See http://www.ifpma.org/documents/NR2204/joint%20position_clinical%20trials.PDF

9 For a copy of the latest edition (Washington, DC 2002; special update Tokyo 2004), see www.wma.net/e/policy/b3.html.

- clinical trials conducted using authorised marketed products in approved indications (Phase IV trials)
- for an authorised product, all clinical trials aimed at developing the product for uses other than those included in the marketing authorisation, e.g., new indications, extensions of existing indications, new patient populations, new dosage forms, new formulations, and comparability studies associated with a change in the manufacturing process.

ii. Compassionate Use and Pre-Approval Patient Access Programmes

Compassionate use and other early pre-approval access programmes (e.g., for orphan drugs) should follow a specific protocol and therefore fall within the scope of the DSUR.

iii. Literature

Any new and significant safety findings from non-clinical and clinical studies that have been published during the period covered by the DSUR should be summarised in the report, including information on products of the same class, and sub-population(s) at risk, where appropriate.

In addition, a commercial sponsor may become aware of new safety information published as an abstract for a scientific meeting. Such information is not readily available to regulatory authorities, and would not be found during literature searches. The Working Group therefore recommends that information from abstracts available to the sponsor that identifies important safety information should be included in the safety evaluation, and a copy of the abstract should be appended to the DSUR. It is recognised that information from such abstracts may be limited and that the sponsor may not be able to obtain additional details.

Although commercial sponsors are expected to review the literature and literature databases (e.g., Medline, EMBASE) periodically for potential new safety information on any of their investigational or marketed products, the CIOMS VII Working Group recognises that this standard may not be appropriate for many non-commercial sponsors. It is anticipated, therefore, that DSURs from non-commercial sponsors may not be comprehensive in this regard.

iv. Other Safety Information

The DSUR should also present and discuss any key findings from other sources as specified below:

Chemistry, Manufacturing and Formulation Issues: The manufacturing process or formulation of an investigational drug may change during the course of clinical development. In such circumstances, any significant identified or potential safety issues arising from these changes should be discussed and evaluated in the DSUR. In particular, the relevant section of the DSUR should include a summary and concise discussion of the following issues, where applicable:

- any significant changes to the manufacturing process introduced during the period covered by the DSUR
- any safety or efficacy findings, or potential concerns, related to a manufacturing (product quality) issue, particularly when the investigational drug is a biologic or biotechnology-derived entity.

Examples of manufacturing issues that could have significant safety implications include container closures, excipients, changes in purification steps, etc.

Non-Clinical Findings: The DSUR should discuss only non-clinical *in vivo* and *in vitro* studies with potential clinical relevance. The results arising from non-clinical studies conducted after the start of the clinical development programme, such as carcinogenicity, reproduction, or immunotoxicity studies, which could have an impact on the clinical safety of the investigational drug, should be summarized in the DSUR. The results of non-clinical studies completed before the start of the clinical development programme will have already been documented in the Investigator Brochure. Generally, they should not be included in the DSUR unless new, potentially significant data become available.

Other Clinical Findings: The DSUR should discuss relevant safety findings from any other available source of clinical safety data (e.g., spontaneous reports, Phase IV studies, or clinical safety data from active surveillance programmes) that might have an impact on the health and well-being of the human subjects enrolled in interventional clinical trials. Such findings could also include unanticipated lack of efficacy results from studies in high morbidity/mortality disease states.

Observational and Epidemiological Studies: When there is continued clinical development of an approved drug, findings from non-interventional studies, such as those using registries, and from epidemiological studies, may have an impact on the benefit-risk assessment for subjects in ongoing clinical trials. Such findings fall within the scope of the DSUR, and should be presented in summary fashion.

(2) Patient Exposure

Data on patient exposure to the investigational drug and comparators help to place adverse event data in context. Ideally, to provide the most meaningful information to assist in the evaluation of clinical safety reports included in the DSUR, patient exposure should be stratified:

- total number of patients in all trials, the number blinded and unblinded, and the numbers known or estimated to be exposed to the investigational drug, placebo and active comparator(s)
- important populations, such as healthy volunteers, patients, or specific sub-populations including children, elderly, renal or hepatic impairment, etc.
- exposure expressed in patient-time (e.g., patient-months or patient-years) is more relevant than a crude number of patients exposed; therefore, the estimation should take into account other variables such as single versus multiple doses, dosage strengths and regimens, length of dosing, dose-modification, and route of administration, if applicable.

While the above scheme represents the ideal situation for presenting patient exposure data, for most development programmes it would not be easily achievable for a DSUR, particularly in the earlier phases of development when many studies are ongoing and remain blinded.

During clinical development, accurate estimation of patient exposure is inherently limited. First, in ongoing trials, the study sponsor is often blinded to the treatment group. Generally this does not pose much of an issue for *exposure*, because the numbers of subjects exposed in a given treatment group can be estimated from the total number of subjects exposed, and the randomisation scheme.[10] Second, there

[10] Blinding is obviously a very significant issue for consideration of causality, when a substantial fraction of the adverse events may have occurred in subjects for whom treatment assignment is unknown. However, this is a different issue and is not covered here.

are delays inherent in processing safety and exposure data from ongoing clinical trials. In some cases, safety and exposure data may be processed through different data systems, and reconciliation and synchronisation of the two datasets are difficult for ongoing trials. When a validated electronic link does not exist between the two systems, denominator data needed to place the summary safety data in perspective will need to be approximated. This situation applies particularly to commercial sponsors.

Therefore, for the purpose of a DSUR, precise numbers of patients exposed to the investigational drug are not routinely expected to be reported. Such figures would only be available to the sponsor when the blind has been broken and when the actual allocation of the patients to the different treatment groups is known (i.e., at the end of the clinical trial when the database has been locked).

Taking into account these difficulties, the CIOMS VII Working Group recommends the following presentation of patient exposure data in the DSUR (see also Chapter III. i.):

- If possible, summary tables should include estimates of the numbers of patients exposed by trial, by time period, and cumulatively during clinical development.
- An estimate of the size of the clinical trial population as of the DSUR data lock point should be provided, using either number of patients or patient-time, if available.
- For a blinded comparative trial, the estimates of patients exposed to the treatment(s) under investigation should be made based on the randomisation scheme.
- The sponsor should clearly explain in the DSUR the method used to calculate or estimate patient exposure.

The data from these tabulations should be placed into context in the overall safety evaluation within the DSUR (see Chapter III.p.).

(3) Presentation and Evaluation of Clinical Trial Data

The DSUR contains both cumulative and interval (periodic) safety information (see also Chapter III.j.(4)).

The interval **line-listings** provide a concise description of the individual suspected, unexpected, serious adverse reactions (SUSARs), as well as suspected unexpected adverse reactions of special interest observed during the period covered by the DSUR.

Cumulative **summary tabulations** of serious adverse events provide a broad overview of the safety profile of the investigational drug (in comparison with the comparators used during the clinical development programme) until a full statistical analysis is performed and the clinical study reports are available.

The report should also include adverse *reactions* of special interest within the line listings and adverse *events* of special interest in summary tabulations (see Glossary for discussion of adverse events/ reactions of special interest). The basis for selection of such events/ reactions should be provided.

i. Interval SUSAR Line Listings

Line listings provide key information on all SUSARs reported during the period covered by the DSUR. They may integrate data across the entire clinical development programme for an investigational drug. Alternatively, when useful and feasible, SUSARs may be listed by protocol, indication, or other variables.

There was considerable discussion within the CIOMS VII Working Group as to the utility of interval line listings in the DSUR, considering that the SUSARs would already have been submitted to regulators on an expedited basis (in some countries in electronic format). Although there were some differences of opinion, several regulators believed there would be value in reviewing information contained in line listings as part of their evaluation of the DSUR. Therefore, the Working Group recommends inclusion of interval SUSAR line listings in the DSUR.

ii. Cumulative Summary Tabulations

Summary tabulations are intended to present cumulative safety data from the clinical programme from the DIBD to the data lock point of the DSUR. Interval summary tabulations are not regarded as particularly useful for this overview presentation. However, judgment will be needed on whether it makes sense to combine serious adverse events from all uses and formulations of the investigational drug, especially after the product is approved and while it is still under development for new uses or with new dosage forms. Separate tabulations would be appropriate in such situations.

As explained in the CIOMS VI Working Group's report, reliance on assessment of individual case causality is of questionable validity in clinical development. Although attribution of causality may be useful for rare ADRs, and for making decisions regarding expedited reporting, the Working Group agreed that it should play a minimal role in the consideration of aggregate data. Thus, the CIOMS VII Working Group recommends that the summary tabulations in a DSUR should include all serious adverse events and not just serious adverse reactions for the investigational drug, as well as for the comparator arm(s) (active comparators, placebo, and treatment unknown due to blinding) used in the programme. As highlighted further in Chapter III, data may be integrated across the programme and separated by trial status (ongoing versus completed).[11] Summary tabulations should include only those terms that were used in defining the case as serious. Non-serious and incidental findings should not be included.

If there are fatal events, those findings should be presented in more detail than might be possible within a summary tabulation (or a line listing). Therefore, a list or tabulation of all fatal events should be included for the latest DSUR interval (not cumulatively) with the following information at a minimum: case number, assigned treatment (may still be blinded), and cause of death. These data should be discussed in the Overall Safety Evaluation section of the DSUR and placed into perspective with respect to the cumulative experience on fatal events.

Among other summary statistics that might be useful for periodic review and reporting are the numbers of patients who dropped out of studies in association with an adverse event. However, for several reasons these data would be difficult to obtain and interpret during an ongoing development programme: most of the data needed are usually found in the clinical trial database, not the safety database; drop-outs are often associated with non-serious events (which would not appear in DSUR line listings or summary tabulations);

---

[11] Sponsors may wish to have the option to prepare additional summary tabulations of serious adverse *reactions* to reflect investigators' assignment of causality; thus, those judged by investigators as not related to study drug, but due to some other cause, would not be included in such a table.

the data may be blinded, especially if the cause were non-serious or the case did not require expedited reporting. Therefore, routine lists or tabulations of drop-outs are not recommended for the DSUR. Comprehensive presentations and analysis of such data will, of course, be submitted with a marketing application at the end of a development programme.

However, when a final analysis or study report is available for one or more trials, or a Data and Safety Monitoring Board (DSMB) has raised drop-outs as an issue (for those programmes using a DSMB), such data should be summarized and discussed within the DSUR.

These recommendations do not preclude the inclusion of a summary of drop-outs, even from ongoing studies, when relevant data are available; this is especially pertinent if there have been medically significant changes from previous DSURs, or new findings that bear on the safety profile or on considerations as to whether there is any question about continuing the studies or programme unaltered.

iii. Results of Completed Studies and Interim Analyses

The DSUR should provide a concise summary of the clinically important safety findings identified from all interventional clinical trials completed during the reporting period (i.e., studies for which a final clinical study report is available; see Appendix 5 for a proposed template).

For interim analyses of ongoing studies, the DSUR should present preliminary findings on: 1) safety issues that are the same or similar to those previously identified in completed studies; and 2) previously unidentified safety signals. The text should be clear as to which of these situations is applicable.

(4) Modifications to Clinical Trial(s)

The DSUR should contain detailed information on the temporary or permanent discontinuation of a clinical trial, or of the clinical development programme for the investigational drug, together with the reasons (apparent lack of efficacy, safety concerns, or commercial reasons). The report should also contain information on any change in the conduct of a trial, protocol, or informed consent information, as well as copies of communications resulting from this type of action, such as Dear Investigator/Doctor Letter(s). A description of any regulatory or DSMB action(s) taken for safety reasons should also be included in the DSUR.

(5) Overall Safety Assessment

The DSUR presents a periodic review and analysis of safety information in order to: 1) examine whether the information reported during the review period is in accord with previous knowledge of the product's safety; 2) identify new safety issues that could have an impact on an individual trial or a development programme, or on the safety of trial subjects; and 3) summarize the status of significant known and potential safety issues. To augment this last objective, and to ensure that focus is placed on what are judged the most significant safety concerns, the CIOMS VII Working Group proposes the inclusion of a summary list of important safety issues, and, when possible, information that is needed to better understand them. Such a list or inventory would be maintained and updated from DSUR to DSUR, and be cumulative, even if an issue had been resolved or fully dealt with (for details, see Chapter III.q.).

For purposes of this ongoing list, the CIOMS Working Group regards a safety issue as "important" if it is thought to rise to the level of what might become a contraindication, warning, or precaution in product information. As defined under EU regulations, an important risk is one that can have an impact on the benefit-risk balance of the product or have implications for public health (see Glossary).

However, as pointed out elsewhere in this CIOMS VII report, the types of data within a DSUR are not adequate or appropriate for conducting an evaluation of the benefit-risk relationship for a product, per se (see Chapter I.c.). Nevertheless, one of the key objectives in the overall evaluation of the data is to judge whether identified or potential risks to the individual patients or study population (subjects already enrolled in a trial as well as those who may be entered in the future) are medically and ethically acceptable when weighed against the demonstrated or anticipated efficacy. In the context of an ongoing development programme, when treatment may be blinded and data have yet to be fully analysed and evaluated, this assessment will necessarily be an approximation, requiring judgment.

As part of this evaluation, a perspective should be given on how risks have been managed, and whether they might be managed better in the future.

III

Development Safety Update Report (DSUR) Model

This Chapter explains what should be included within each section of the proposed DSUR. The material is presented in the order in which the sections should appear in an actual report. As will become clear, the DSUR contains separate sections for presentation of the relevant data, analyses and interpretation of the data, recommended actions, and conclusions. To ensure efficient and clear presentation of information in a DSUR, sponsors should avoid unnecessary duplication of material within the different sections of the report. Sample DSURs for commercial and non-commercial sponsors for fictitious products can be found in Appendix 4.

The Appendices specified for the model DSUR itself are found at the end of this chapter so as to distinguish them from the appendices referred to as part of this CIOMS VII report overall.

a. Title Page

The DSUR title page should specify the following:

- the document type and number (e.g., Development Safety Update Report #2)
- investigational drug
- sponsor name and address
- the review period
- Development International Birth Date (DIBD)
- date of the report
- a statement on confidentiality of the data as a footnote (see sample DSURs for an example, Appendix 4)

b. Table of Contents

Executive Summary
1. Introduction
2. Worldwide Marketing Authorisation Status (if applicable)
3. Update on Actions Taken for Safety Reasons
4. Changes to Reference Safety Information
5. Inventory and Status of Ongoing and Completed Interventional Clinical Trials

6. Estimated Patient Exposure in Clinical Trials
7. Presentation of Safety Data from Clinical Studies
    7.1 Sources of Clinical Study Data
    7.2 General Considerations
    7.3 Line Listings
    7.4 Summary Tabulations
        7.4.1 General Considerations
        7.4.2 Presentations of Summary Tabulations
        7.4.3 Summary Tabulations for Combination Therapies
8. Significant Findings from Interventional Clinical Trials
9. Observational and Epidemiological Studies
10. Other Information
    10.1 Lack of Efficacy
    10.2 Chemistry, Manufacturing, and Formulation Issues
    10.3 Non-Clinical Findings
    10.4 Literature
11. Information from Marketing Experience
12. Late Breaking Information
13. Overall Safety Evaluation
    13.1 Evaluation of the Risks
    13.2 Benefit versus Risk Considerations
14. Summary of Important Risks
15. New Actions Recommended
16. Conclusions

Appendices to DSUR

Appendix A: Inventory of Ongoing and Completed Interventional Clinical Trials
Appendix B: DCSI or Safety Sections of IB Available at Beginning of Report Period
Appendix C: Line Listing(s)
Appendix D: Cumulative Summary Tabulation(s)
Appendix E: Summary Tabulations by Selected Parameters (e.g., indication, formulation, patient population, etc.)

c. Executive Summary

The sponsor should present a brief overview (no more than two pages) to provide regulators with a description of the most important information contained within the DSUR. This summary can also be provided to other stakeholders as discussed in Chapter II. The executive summary should highlight any important, identified safety issues for the investigational drug, the impact on study populations, and any regulatory or sponsor action(s) taken or proposed.

This Executive Summary should not be used as the usual cover letter for submission of the DSUR, because the latter is generated locally and may have to be country-specific.

d. Introduction

This section should include the following:

- identification of the report as a DSUR, the number of the report, and the review period covered
- a brief description of the investigational drug under study (e.g., new chemical entity, biotechnology-derived product, vaccine, etc.). Also, the drug class, putative mechanism of action, dosage form(s), formulation(s), and route(s) of administration should be described.
- whether the DSUR is for a single study (e.g., as might be the case for a non-commercial sponsor) or for a development programme (commercial sponsor). It is important to describe which interventional trials are included (e.g., all trials for the programme or indication-specific trials).
- a brief summary of the objectives of the clinical development plan and ongoing clinical trials, specifying indications and treated population(s)
- If the product has been granted marketing approval, provide a brief summary of the marketing authorisation status. Details should be included in Section e., below.
- a brief description of any particular data excluded. Exclusions should be explained; for example, they may be covered in a separate periodic safety report by a licensing partner under conditions which do not allow for a single report by both parties.

In line with the ICH E2C guideline for Periodic Safety Update Reports (PSURs) for marketed products, and as explained in Chapter II, the CIOMS VII Working Group recommends preparation and submission of a single DSUR for a single product. If there is clear evidence that the safety profile of the investigational drug is formulation, indication, or population specific, separate data presentations may be appropriate within the single DSUR. However, there may be exceptional situations for which completely separate DSURs are more appropriate or practical. See Chapter II.a.(8).

For investigational drugs being co-developed by more than one party (more than one commercial interest, or a commercial interest plus a non-commercial sponsor), the CIOMS VII Working Group recommends preparation of a single DSUR by one of the parties, whenever possible. The DSUR should state *what* is included (i.e., whether the safety data from other commercial or non-commercial entities are included in the report, or in a separate report prepared by a third party). The logistics describing exchange of safety information between parties should be included in the report. For non-commercial sponsors who have to submit their own DSUR to a regulatory authority, their data could still be included in the commercial sponsor's global DSUR, with a suitable explanation.

In circumstances when separate reports must be provided by different partners due to limitations imposed by contractual agreements (for example, co-development of one indication only, while additional indications are being investigated by the other company), the respective DSURs should delineate clearly the scope of the data included in the separate reports.

e. Worldwide Marketing Authorisation Status

This section is applicable only if a marketing application for a product has been approved or rejected by regulatory authorities in one or more countries or regions. The information provided, usually as a table, should be cumulative. The information required for this section is virtually the same as that required for a PSUR (ICH Guideline E2C), which can be consulted for a suggested table format to summarize the data.[1]

The following information should be provided for each country or region where marketing authorisation has been obtained:

- date(s) of marketing authorisation
- any qualifications surrounding the authorisation, such as limits on indications if relevant to safety

[1] See www.ich.org/LOB/media/MEDIA477.pdf for the latest version of ICH E2C.

- treatment indications, dosage form(s), and special populations covered by the marketing authorisation(s), when relevant
- date(s) of launch if known
- trade name(s) for the product
- lack of approval by regulatory authorities, including an explanation (e.g., lack of efficacy, safety issue[s], additional manufacturing information needed, etc.)
- withdrawal by the sponsor of a licence application submission if related to safety or efficacy.

Typically, indications for use, populations treated, and dosage forms will be the same in the majority of countries where the product is authorised. However, when there are important differences, such information should be noted. The table may be used to highlight the differences between countries/regions. This is particularly important when there are meaningful differences in safety data between regions, which may be related to dissimilarities in exposure or use. If convenient and useful, separate regulatory status tables may be appropriate for different product uses or forms.

Countries granting marketing authorisations should be listed in chronological order (the earliest first). For multiple authorisations in one or more countries (e.g., new dosage forms), the International Birth Date (IBD) for an active substance covered by a PSUR, and therefore the Development International Birth Date (DIBD), should be the first (initial) authorisation date. For details, see Chapter II.a.(6).

f. Update on Actions Taken for Safety Reasons

This section should include a description of significant actions related to safety which have already been taken by the sponsor, regulators, DSMBs or Independent Ethics Committees (IECs), which may have an impact on the conduct of a specific trial or the whole development plan (e.g., non-approval of a trial or a delay in a decision to approve a clinical trial due to a safety concern). This does not apply to a delay in a response to an application or approval by an IEC due to logistical reasons; such delays are considered irrelevant information. Examples of significant actions include:

- partial or complete clinical trial suspension
- hold or early termination of clinical trial due to lack of efficacy or safety issues
- removal of a clinical hold
- protocol modifications due to safety or efficacy concerns (e.g., dosage changes, changes in study entrance criteria, intensification of monitoring, etc.)
- changes in target population or indications
- changes to the Informed Consent document
- formulation changes
- failure to obtain marketing authorization for a tested indication
- significant changes to the Development Risk Management Plan (e.g., addition of a special reporting requirement, issuance of a Dear Investigator or Dear Doctor letter, plans for new safety studies including PASS [Post-Authorization Safety Studies, as required by some regulators], etc.).

In addition, for products already marketed, the following information should be addressed:

- failure to obtain a marketing authorization renewal (e.g., in the EU)
- marketing authorization withdrawal or suspension for safety reasons
- restrictions on distribution
- significant changes in labelling documents such as indication or population restriction, Black Box Warning, etc.

The safety-related reasons that led to these actions should be described. For example, a contraindication or warning may be requested by a regulatory agency even if not agreed to by the company. Communications with the health care profession as a result of such action should also be described, and documentation should be made available and provided upon request.

Changes to the DCSI or Investigator Brochure should be discussed separately in section g.

g. Changes to Reference Safety Information

This section should specify whether or not any significant changes were made to the Development Core Safety Information (DCSI) or safety sections of the Investigator Brochure (IB) during the review period. The version in effect at the beginning of the period covered by the report should be attached as Appendix B, and will be used as the reference safety document.

Significant changes to any of the following sections of the DCSI/IB are appropriate for discussion in this section: contraindications, precautions, warnings, ADRs, adverse reactions of special interest, or interactions. New precautionary measures (e.g., periodic liver function tests or ECG monitoring) should be discussed as well. Important findings, positive or negative, from animal or *in vitro* studies also warrant discussion here (e.g., carcinogenicity studies; hERG studies).

Minor amendments made as part of the periodic review and update of the DCSI or IB need not be described. Addition of non-serious adverse reactions from completed trials should be listed briefly.

If the investigational drug was granted marketing approval in one or more countries or regions during the period covering the current DSUR, it may be appropriate to highlight and explain any major differences between the DCSI/IB and the Company Core Safety Information (CCSI).

h. Inventory and Status of Ongoing and Completed Interventional Clinical Trials

This section of the report provides cumulative information. It should refer to an Appendix table that presents a cumulative list of ongoing and completed interventional clinical trials (Phases I-IV), as well as compassionate use studies.

The following information for each trial should be provided (see Appendix A for an example):

- protocol number or other trial identifier[2]
- clinical trial phase (I, II, III, IV)
- status:
  - ongoing (study has begun; study has begun but currently on hold; study is completed, but final clinical study report is not yet available)
  - completed (final clinical study report available)

[2] Commercial sponsors may wish to include the EU EUDRACT trial number in addition to their internal trial code.

- names of countries in which there is at least one investigative site for the protocol
- study title (abbreviated if necessary)
- study design (single blind, open, double blind, parallel, crossover, etc., including treatment arms and duration)
- dose and regimen of study drug and any control treatments
- subject population (sex, age, indication[s], specific patient groups [e.g., patients with impaired renal function, patients resistant to treatment, etc.])
- Date of First Visit for First Patient (FVFP)
- planned enrolment
- estimates of interval and cumulative numbers of exposed patients for each treatment arm, presented by protocol. The actual enrolment numbers for open or completed trials, or an estimate based on the randomisation scheme for blinded trials, should be included. Presentation by indication, formulation, and population should be provided, if applicable.

i. Estimated Patient Exposure in Clinical Trials

Exposure data, a function of numbers of subjects and time-on-study, provide the necessary context for interpretation of adverse events. For a single randomised controlled trial, where mean time-on-study is similar for each treatment group, direct comparisons of the numbers of adverse events in each study group can be informative, because time is common to all groups. However, the majority of development programmes are more complex, and subject exposure (numbers of subjects and time) often varies by study, treatment group, dose, patient population, and indication. Thus, the DSUR should provide approximations of numbers of subjects exposed, and when possible time on study, by treatment group (unknown [blinded trial], investigational drug, comparator, and placebo arms), and by study. When possible, exposure should be estimated as median time on study, or presented as the approximate percentage of subjects who have been exposed for a particular length of time (e.g., 78% of subjects have had ≥ one year exposure).

For blinded comparative trials, the sponsor should estimate the numbers of patients exposed to the investigational treatments based on the randomisation scheme (e.g., in trials with a 1:1:1 distribution of patients, the approximate patient exposure to each group would be one third of the total number of patients enrolled). For open trials, or completed and unblinded trials, the DSUR should provide reasonably accurate figures.

When the pattern of case reports suggests a potential problem, a further stratification for relevant population categories such as age, gender, country, dose, indication, formulation, or population can also be calculated and presented as needed.

j. Presentation of Safety Data from Clinical Studies

(1) Sources of Clinical Study Data

This section of the DSUR will incorporate clinical trial data from:

- all completed and ongoing interventional studies, including Phase I through Phase IV, as appropriate. This includes published interventional studies.[3]
- clinical trial data from studies conducted by co-development partners in a licensing agreement (if the scope of the licensing agreement allows for this)
- data from sponsored Compassionate Use and pre-approval special access programmes, if applicable.

The CIOMS VII Working Group recommends one DSUR for each investigational drug. Thus, information from all sources should be combined into a single DSUR, when possible. However, when data from clinical studies not sponsored by the author of a DSUR are not obtainable, they will have to be submitted in separate DSURs by the different sponsors.

(2) General Considerations

The purpose of this section of the DSUR is to present important clinical safety data in two ways:

- interval line listings of specific types of adverse reactions that arose during the period covered by the current DSUR

[3] When including data from completed studies which have been published, it is important that this information is not duplicated elsewhere in the DSUR without appropriate cross reference.

- summary tabulations of cumulative data that have arisen since initiation of the first trial (since the DIBD).

The routine inclusion of individual case narratives from clinical studies is not recommended. The DSUR represents primarily a descriptive summary; it does not have the precision of a clinical study report or the completeness of an Integrated Safety Summary submitted at the time of a marketing application.

For extensive development programmes, serious adverse events (SAEs) presented in the summary tabulations will be reported from ongoing interventional clinical trials as well as completed studies, and may contain both blinded and unblinded information. In order to preserve the integrity of ongoing studies, CIOMS Working Group VII anticipates that only cases qualifying for expedited reporting will have been unblinded (i.e., serious, unexpected and suspected adverse drug reactions, and possibly adverse reactions of special interest that may not be serious).

In addition, certain events may be excluded from the summary tabulations and line listings. Examples of such adverse events include those which:

- have been defined in the protocol as "exempt" from special collection and entry into the safety database, e.g., disease progression in cancer studies, Kaposi's sarcoma in HIV studies, etc.
- are integral to efficacy endpoints, e.g., deaths reported in a trial of a drug for congestive heart failure, wherein all-cause mortality is the primary efficacy endpoint.

All such exclusions should be explained in the report.

For commercial sponsors with separate clinical and safety database systems (or departments), SAE reconciliation may occur on an ongoing basis, or only at the end of the study. Therefore, some of the data in the DSUR may be based on preliminary information from ongoing studies and may not have been validated or reconciled. The analyses need to be interpreted with these considerations in mind.

(3) Line Listings

DSUR line listings should be provided for both the investigational compound and active comparator(s), and should consist of the following information:

- unblinded suspected, unexpected and serious ADRs (SUSARs), and adverse reactions of special interest if they were reported on an expedited basis
- cases which have been identified during the period covered by the DSUR (interval data)
- integrated data across the programme or split by protocol, indication, or other important variables, as appropriate.

The principles, content and format recommended in the CIOMS II report and in ICH Guideline E2C for PSUR line listings can be used with appropriate modification (e.g., inclusion of the clinical trial identification number/code). It may be appropriate to include only one set of line listings covering the entire clinical trial programme, subdivided by treatment assignment. However, depending on the nature of the programme and the number of cases, separate listings may be presented, when appropriate and relevant, by protocol, formulation/dosage form, indication, or route of administration. An example of a typical line listing format and content is presented in Appendix C to this chapter, and in Appendix 4 (sample DSUR) at the end of this report.

(4) Summary Tabulations

i. General Considerations

The purpose of the summary tabulation(s) is to present the current status of cumulative serious adverse event cases for the clinical development programme and to support the analysis and commentary elsewhere in the DSUR. The summary tabulation is considered to be a core element of the data presentation, and hence should be included in all DSURs, unless there are very few reported serious events, when an overall narrative description may be more suitable. Summary tabulations should be presented by treatment arm, unless treatment assignment is unknown (remains blinded).

If "adverse events of special interest" have been included in the summary tabulations, they should be identified as such and explained.

Summary tabulation(s) should:

- be cumulative throughout all DSURs for the drug
- contain all serious adverse **events** (not just reactions) from interventional clinical trials, including signs, symptoms or

diagnoses. Multiple SAEs experienced by a single subject should be included separately. For example, if a case report from a clinical study is received which includes medically distinct SAEs, such as hepatitis, pneumonia, and cardiac failure, then these terms would be captured separately although they were reported in only one patient.

- contain diagnoses, where available, rather than the individual signs and symptoms. However, in the absence of a diagnosis, the individual signs and symptoms should be presented (e.g., abdominal swelling, nausea)
- present events separately by treatment arm (placebo, comparator, or blinded therapy)
- clearly identify terms that were unlisted in the DCSI/IB at the beginning of the period. Although the DCSI/IB may have been updated during the period to make such events listed (and the changes should be noted in section g. of the DSUR), highlighting them in the tabulations would provide a snapshot of new information.
- make use of the sponsor's most recent version of MedDRA.

The standard cumulative summary tabulation should consist of the following:

- Number of adverse event terms for each body system (System Organ Class, SOC) that were used to define the case as serious.
- Terms expressed at the MedDRA Preferred Term Level. There may be occasions when High Level Group Terms are more appropriate.[4]

An example of a cumulative Summary Tabulation is provided in Appendix D at the end of this chapter and in Appendix 4 at the end of this report.

ii. Presentation of Summary Tabulations

As a general rule, SAE data from all sponsored studies in a particular indication should be integrated across all interventional trials in a development programme. In certain circumstances,

[4] See the MedDRA Points to Consider document: http://www.ich.org/LOB/media/MEDIA2837.pdf

however, separate summary tabulations may be more appropriate for adequate presentation of the data, and to support the conclusions within the DSUR. This is especially true when different indications, populations or formulations are being studied with the same investigational drug. Separate tabulations are also important to consider when, for example, SAEs appear to be related to a particular protocol, or study procedure or design, or where they have led to a change in the conduct of the study (e.g., change in dose, suspension or closure of the trial, significant changes in the informed consent document). If the data are sufficient and suggestive, it may also be useful to present SAE tabulations as a function of baseline demographic characteristics (e.g., ethnicity, race, etc.).

The number and design of separate summary tabulations are matters of clinical and scientific judgement, but should be planned according to the specific effects of the given investigational drug, as well as the stage and nature of the development programme.

Separate tabulations may therefore be considered for the following circumstances:

- different indications (e.g., a dopamine agonist that is developed simultaneously for treatment of Parkinson's Disease and for prolactin-secreting pituitary adenomas)
- different patient populations (e.g., an investigational drug studied in the same indication for adults, adults with renal insufficiency, and children)
- different pharmaceutical formulations (e.g., when an immediate release and an extended release formulation are in simultaneous development)
- different routes of administration (e.g., intravenous and oral)
- duration of exposure (separation by duration of exposure can help characterise events with longer latency; combining groups with disparate exposures may obfuscate these events)
- different doses (e.g., all SAEs can be shown by dose in the same tabulation)

- different trials (protocols), if considered scientifically appropriate (e.g., if certain SAEs are thought to be directly related to protocol procedures or a specific study design)
- by country of origin, if scientifically relevant.

Separate tabulations may also be considered for SAE data available to the sponsor from trials conducted by independent sponsor-investigators, where appropriate (e.g., if a new, clinically significant safety issue has been identified from a trial or trials not sponsored by the preparer of the DSUR).

When more than one summary tabulation is considered appropriate, the organization of the tabulations should be outlined and the rationale should be provided.

Examples of Summary Tabulations for some of the above situations are presented in Appendix E.

iii. Summary Tabulations for Combination Therapies

For protocols or programmes involving combination therapies (e.g., treatments in the HIV or oncology therapeutic areas), the CIOMS VII Working Group recommends presentation of the SAE data for the combination of therapies as opposed to attempting to associate the SAEs with an individual product in the combination, especially if the specific combination is planned to be submitted for marketing approval. This principle applies for fixed combination products as well. For trials with factorial designs, involving comparisons between the combination and its individual components, the SAEs for the individual comparators and combination should be shown.

k. Significant Findings from Interventional Clinical Trials

The focus of this section is on the summarisation of clinically important safety findings that have been identified from completed and ongoing sponsored interventional studies during the period covered by the DSUR, as well as from compassionate use studies and trials from co-development programmes, as appropriate. New analyses or interpretations of previously reported data should also be incorporated. However, findings related to lack of efficacy should be discussed in a different section (see m.(1), below).

Prior to any marketing authorisation of the investigational drug, this section will summarise data only from completed and ongoing studies in unapproved indications, dosage forms, populations, and other uses. Following authorisation in any market and with the conduct of Phase IV trials, this section should contain information from studies in both approved and unapproved indications.

The section should include:

- a brief synopsis of significant findings from each **completed** study or from any **interim analyses** conducted in the period covered by the DSUR, with a focus on any key safety findings. Examples of significant medical findings would include evidence of hepatotoxicity, cardiovascular effects, significant hypersensitivity, or immunogenicity. The discussion should include a concise description of the issue or safety signal, highlighting any identified risk factors, evidence of a dose-related effect, and other relevant information. Appendix 5 provides a template for a study synopsis. If no new safety findings have been identified, this should be stated.

- for ongoing studies, a discussion of any preliminary safety findings, either those consistent with issues already identified in completed studies, or early evidence of new, clinically important safety signals requiring further clarification.

- safety data relevant to combination therapies, when an investigational drug is co-administered with a licensed drug product or device (e.g., administration of an investigational thrombolytic agent with a marketed platelet glycoprotein IIb/IIIa inhibitor; studies where a device is required to administer an investigational drug). New safety data relevant to the co-administered product or device may affect the overall risk of study participation, and should be described.

The level of discussion will depend on the authorship of the DSUR. As a general rule, commercial (pharmaceutical company) sponsors are likely to have a much broader overview of the issues in the context of a development programme. This would also apply to non-commercial centres that sponsor extensive study programmes. For most non-commercial/academic sponsors, the discussion is likely to be at an individual study level and hence of a more limited nature.

l. Observational and Epidemiological Studies

This section should include a summary of clinically relevant findings or findings pertinent to the development programme from epidemiological and observational studies completed during the period covered by the DSUR (e.g., case control studies, or studies using automated databases in locations where the investigational product is already on the market). Significant findings from interim analyses of observational and epidemiological studies should be included in this section as well.

In the pre-approval period, epidemiology studies are sometimes conducted to characterise the natural history of the disease being investigated, in order to place reported events into the context of the background prevalence. When the results of these studies add to the understanding of the natural history and significant background adverse event profile in the population, the findings should be concisely summarised.

As with other types of potentially useful information, significant results (from the literature, for example) of observational and epidemiological studies with drugs in the same class as the investigational product should also be included if they have an important bearing on safety.

m. Other Information

(1) Lack of Efficacy

For products intended to treat serious or life-threatening diseases, data suggesting lack of efficacy may constitute a significant risk of study participation, and should be reported in this section (e.g., in trials investigating a new treatment for sepsis, new evidence of higher mortality than previously observed due to lack of efficacy).

(2) Chemistry, Manufacturing and Formulation Issues

Significant manufacturing or microbiological changes implemented subsequent to submission of the most recent DSUR should be summarized (e.g., changes in raw materials, the formulation of the investigational drug, the manufacturing process or excipients). In addition, the sponsor should concisely assess the potential impact of any changes introduced with respect to safety and efficacy, and the continued development of the investigational drug.

(3) Non-Clinical Findings

This section should include potentially significant findings from non-clinical studies, either in progress, or completed subsequent to submission of the most recent DSUR. Such investigations can include:

- *in vitro* studies (e.g., drug interaction studies, mutagenicity, genotoxicity, hERG studies)
- animal studies (e.g., pharmacology, pharmacokinetics, acute and chronic toxicology, reproductive toxicology, carcinogenicity, immunogenicity).

(4) Literature

Clinical and non-clinical data published in the scientific and medical literature in the period covered by the DSUR should be summarized if relevant and important to the safety of the investigational drug, including information in abstracts from scientific meetings. Copies of such abstracts should be included in the DSUR, but copies of published papers should be submitted only on request. It is important that information on any published study which has already been included as a synopsis as described in Section k is not duplicated but appropriately cross-referenced.

n. Information from Marketing Experience

For products that have been approved in one or more countries, this section should include a concise summary of key safety findings that have arisen from marketing experience, especially if they have been associated with amendments to the prescribing information, core data sheet, Investigator's Brochure or informed consent document; have led to regulatory action; or have resulted in amendments to the Risk Management Plan for the product.

If available, it would be appropriate to include the Executive Summary from the most recent PSUR in this section.

o. Late Breaking Information

This section should be reserved for new information that was received (or generated) after the data lock point for the DSUR, and too late to be integrated into all of the appropriate section(s) of the report. Examples include clinically significant new case reports, important follow-up data, clinically relevant toxicological findings, as well as any definitive action that may have been taken by the sponsor, a Data and Safety Monitoring Board, or regulatory authority for safety reasons. Although the information will not be represented in its appropriate section of the DSUR, it should be taken into account in the Overall Safety Evaluation.

p. Overall Safety Evaluation

The overall safety evaluation should provide a concise, integrated appraisal of new non-clinical, clinical, and epidemiological information relative to previous knowledge of the investigational drug. This assessment should consider both cumulative experience and new information collected in the period covered by the DSUR. The analysis will also include an assessment of the implications (if any) for the clinical trial population, as well as the intended or actual population for the approved product, as appropriate. This section should not reiterate or summarise data and information presented in previous sections, but should be presented as an **interpretation** of those data.

If new and relevant follow-up information was received on a safety issue identified in a previous periodic report, it should be discussed in this section to allow further clarification of the issue, irrespective of whether the information supports a positive or negative finding.

For products in clinical development for multiple indications or populations, or with different dosage forms, consideration of the overall safety evaluation by subgroup is a matter of medical judgment.

In early phases of a development programme, data will be inherently limited. However, when new and more extensive information is available, a broader and more comprehensive assessment is possible. The sources of the information should be clearly identified.

(1) Evaluation of the Risks

The following points from all available clinical sources should be discussed:

- meaningful changes in characteristics of previously identified (listed) reactions (e.g., frequency or severity, outcome, specific or new at-risk population[s])
- for newly identified safety issues, describe the type of adverse reaction in detail, associated laboratory values, the mechanism of injury

(when known), the identification of potential risk factors and the relationship of ADRs to relevant parameters (e.g., dose, deviation from treatment protocol, duration of treatment); parameters that could be useful in predicting or preventing ADRs are of particular interest

- particular emphasis should be placed on symptoms, signs, and laboratory evidence of newly and previously identified, clinically significant:
  - hepatotoxicity
  - cardiovascular effects, including QTc interval prolongation
  - bone marrow toxicity
  - renal toxicity
  - central nervous system toxicity
  - immunogenicity and hypersensitivity
  - reactive metabolites
- all deaths which are an outcome of any suspected adverse reaction
- evidence of reversibility
- evidence or potential for pharmacokinetic or pharmacodynamic interactions (including drug-drug and food-drug interactions)
- reasons for patient withdrawals due to safety reasons including abnormal laboratory values, investigations such as ECGs or other adverse events (however, see Chapter II.b.(3).ii.)
- overdose (deliberate or inadvertent) and its treatment
- drug misuse or abuse
- positive or negative experiences with use in pregnancy or lactation
- experience in special patient groups (e.g., children, elderly, hepatic or renal impairment)
- experience with long-term treatment
- risks that may be associated with the conduct or design of a trial
- potential impact of new safety issues identified with another drug in the same class (e.g., from literature sources)
- evidence of clinically significant medication errors
- areas identified as those of special medical interest (e.g., impact on growth and development with use of drugs for paediatric indications)

- specific safety issues associated with combination therapies or drug-device combinations.

In addition, the following points should be considered:

- significant manufacturing and microbiological changes with potential safety implications
- non–clinical safety findings with potential human relevance (e.g., toxicology, general pharmacology, and *in vitro* drug interaction data).

(2) Benefit Versus Risk Considerations

The sponsor should provide a perspective on the balance between identified risks and anticipated efficacy/benefits as it pertains to the individual study participants and the study population in general (i.e., trial programme). In particular, the sponsor should assess whether the information obtained since the previous DSUR suggests a significant change in this balance. If it is judged that the balance has changed, the sponsor should provide an assessment of the impact on the clinical development programme.

This perspective is particularly important and should be addressed in all DSURs. In many respects, it represents the culmination of the evaluation and helps the sponsor and the DSUR recipients to judge whether there is any reason to consider modification or even discontinuation of one or more studies, or a development programme, in the interest of study participant safety. This consideration should be brought forward to the Conclusions section of the DSUR (see s., below).

q. Summary of Important Risks

This section should include a cumulative list of newly or previously identified (known) or potential important risks along with information that might be helpful to clarify a specific safety issue, or to gain better understanding of the safety profile of the product. The summary should include only medically important risks, such as those that might be expected to become contraindications, warnings, and precautions in labelling (e.g., hepatotoxicity, renal toxicity, cardiovascular effects including QTc interval prolongation, bone marrow toxicity, drug-drug interactions, immunogenicity, and hypersensitivity). The selection of issues will require judgement and may be based on uncommon but important items unique to the product or its class, or on adverse events of special interest. This is the type of information that might be specified in a company's Development Risk Management Plan or in the Safety Specification of the Pharmacovigilance/Risk Management Plan at the time of submission of the marketing authorisation application, as defined under ICH Guideline E2E and proposed in the CIOMS VI report. As such, this section forms a common link between the DSUR, DRMP, and post-approval Risk Management Plan.

Each item on the list should be accompanied by a brief discussion summarizing the status of the issue. Examples from consecutive fictitious DSURs over a four-year period are shown below; other examples are found in Appendix 4.[5]

Summary of Important Risks (DSUR 2007)

1. Hepatotoxicity. In study RAT-001, 9 of 12 rats that received the highest dose of Drug 123 (500 mg/kg) developed transaminase elevations; focal hepatic necrosis was observed in three rats. There were equivocal findings of hepatic toxicity in canine study DOG001. Some of the other drugs in the class have been associated with hepatic toxicity. The ongoing Phase I study includes weekly monitoring of transaminases, bilirubin, and alkaline phosphatase, and the risk of hepatotoxicity is delineated in the informed consent document. To date, there have been no AEs of hepatic toxicity. Toxicity is being further characterised in a second canine study (DOG002).

Summary of Important Risks (DSUR 2008)

1. Hepatotoxicity. This class of drugs is associated with hepatic toxicity, which is generally mild and reversible. High doses of Drug 123 were associated with hepatic injury in a non-clinical rat study, and there were equivocal findings of hepatic toxicity in a canine study (DOG001). In a second canine study (DOG002), there were no significant transaminase elevations at doses up to 200 mg/kg. Histological analyses are pending. Subjects in the single-dose Phase I study were monitored with weekly transaminases through 6 weeks, and none experienced significant transaminase elevations (36 subjects exposed to single doses ≥ 50 mg/kg). Nevertheless, for the ongoing repeat-dose Phase II study, liver function tests are being obtained every two weeks, and the informed consent document includes language regarding hepatotoxicity.

[5] Even if an issue or signal included in this section is eventually shown to be false or unimportant, or if shown to be real and has been resolved and reflected in product information, it should remain in this cumulative inventory throughout the life of the DSUR cycle, albeit in abbreviated form.

Summary of Important Risks (DSUR 2009)

1. Hepatotoxicity. This class of drugs is associated with hepatic toxicity, which is generally mild and reversible. There was initial evidence of hepatic injury (focal hepatic necrosis) in rats exposed to high doses of Drug 123 (500 mg/kg). In two subsequent studies, dogs exposed to lower doses did not have evidence of hepatic toxicity. In the Phase I study (36 subjects received a single dose, up to 50 mg/kg), there were no significant transaminase elevations. The phase II repeat-dose studies ("CUREIT" and "DEPEND") have not raised concerns regarding hepatic injury (*see: Significant Findings from Interventional Clinical Trials*). Although the ongoing DEPEND study remains blinded, there have been no SAEs suggestive of hepatic toxicity, with 79 of the planned 160 subjects enrolled.

Summary of Important Risks (DSUR 2010)

1. Hepatotoxicity. This class of drugs is associated with hepatic toxicity, which is generally mild and reversible. There was equivocal evidence of hepatic injury in rats exposed to high-dose Drug 123 (500 mg/kg); there was no evidence of hepatic toxicity in two canine studies. Similarly, the concern has not been borne out in the Phase I or II studies (*see: Significant Findings from Interventional Clinical Trials*). For the ongoing Phase III study, transaminases are being evaluated every 4 weeks (X 2), then every month (X 2), then every three months. For the three treatment groups overall, there have been twelve AEs for hepatic toxicity, with approximately 210 subjects enrolled. The DSMB is aware of, and is monitoring, this issue.

r. New Actions Recommended

This section should include a description of significant actions proposed by the sponsor, or requested by one or more regulatory authorities, but not yet implemented. This section is not meant to include actions that have already been taken, as described in section f. above. Such actions may be (or may have been) proposed by the sponsor, regulators, safety monitoring committees, or independent ethics committees (IECs), and could have an impact on the conduct of a specific trial or the whole development plan. For example, the following information should be provided if under consideration but not yet implemented:

- non-approval of a trial or a delay in a decision to approve a clinical trial due to a safety concern (This does not apply to a delay in a response to an application or approval by an IEC due to logistical or administrative reasons.)

- partial or complete clinical trial suspension/hold, or early termination of a clinical trial due to safety issues or lack of efficacy
- removal of a clinical hold
- protocol modification(s) due to significant efficacy or safety concerns, including non-clinical findings that may have an impact on human exposure (e.g., dosage changes, addition of ECG measurements, etc.)
- protocol amendments to add new instructions to investigators to report events of special interest according to the Serious Adverse Event reporting timeframe
- revisions to the informed consent document
- pending changes to the DCSI
- changes in target population or indications
- formulation or manufacturing changes
- significant changes to the Development Risk Management Plan (e.g., addition of a special reporting requirement)
- issuance of a Dear Investigator alert letter
- plans for new studies related to safety issues (e.g., mechanistic, pharmacokinetic, etc.).

When relevant, any proposed actions related to the status of marketing authorization applications that are described in section e., above, should be cross-referenced here.

In addition, for products with an existing marketing authorisation, the following information should be provided, if under consideration but not yet implemented:

- restrictions on product distribution
- significant changes to the Reference Safety Information, such as indication or population restrictions, precautions, warnings, contra-indications, etc.
- issuance of a Dear Doctor letter

- plans for new safety studies including PASS (Post-Authorisation Safety Studies, as required by some regulators).

The safety-related reasons for the proposed or requested actions should be described. For example, a contraindication or warning may be requested by one regulatory agency even if not agreed to by the company; any proposed communication with the health care profession as a result of such action should also be described and documentation should be provided upon request.

s. Conclusions

The conclusions section should be brief and reflect on the totality of the cumulative experience:

- indicate which safety data are no longer consistent with the experience described in previous periodic reports and with the Reference Safety Information (DCSI, safety sections of the IB, and CCSI, if relevant)
- highlight any significant changes in observed risk in relation to anticipated benefit
- on the basis of the data, indicate changes that should be, or have been, made to improve management of risk, if applicable
- include a statement by the sponsor that actions taken or recommended, as described in sections f. and r., above, will either:

1) justify unaltered continuation of the development programme;
2) warrant modification of the trial(s) or programme to better manage risk; or
3) necessitate suspension of a trial(s) or programme, as appropriate.

Appendix A

Inventory of Ongoing and Completed Interventional Clinical Trials

Two sample tables are presented here to show how different indications for the same product might be handled.

Project name: ____________
Formulation: XX (Capsules)
Indication: Hypertension

Study ID Phase Status	Countries	Study Title	Design, Duration of Treatment	Dose and Regimen of Study Therapy(ies)	Subject Population	FVFP* and Planned Enrolment	Interval/ Cumulative Enrolment	Interval/ Cumulative Patient Exposure per Treatment Arm
XX-2476 Phase II Completed	UK, DE, FR	Assessment of safety and efficacy in patients with severe hypertension	Randomised, double-blind, parallel, placebo-controlled 4 Weeks	XX: 30 mg OD Placebo OD	Females/ males Age: 18-60 Severe hypertension	01 Jun 2004 222	64/222	XX 30mg: 32/111 Placebo: 32/111
XX-2666 Phase III Ongoing	UK	Long-term efficacy and safety in elderly patients suffering from mild to moderate hyper-tension	Open-label, 2 Years	XX: 15 mg OD XX: 30 mg OD	Females/ males Age: >60 Elderly; impaired renal function	01 March 2005 300	42/112	XX 15mg: 21/56 XX 30mg: 21/56
TOTAL						**522**	**106/334**	**XX 15mg: 21/56** **XX 30mg: 53/167** **Placebo: 32/111**

* FVFP = First Visit First Patient

Project name: ___________
Formulation: XX (Capsules)
Indication: Congestive Heart Failure

Study ID Phase Status	Countries	Study Title	Design Duration of Treatment	Dose and Regimen of Study Therapy(ies)	Subject Population	FVFP* Planned Enrolment	Interval/ Cumulative Enrolment	Interval/ Cumulative patient Exposure per Treatment Arm
XX 3184 Phase II Ongoing	USA, UK, CA	Assessment of safety and efficacy in patients with severe congestive heart failure	Randomised, double blind, parallel, placebo controlled, 12 Weeks	XX: 7.5 mg OD Comparator: 100 mg OD Placebo OD	Females/ males Age:18-60 ejection fraction ≤ 0.40	31 Dec 2005 180	30/60	XX : 7.5mg: 10/20 Comparator: 100 mg 10/20 Placebo: 10/20
TOTAL						**180**	**30/60**	**XX 7.5mg: 10/20** **Comparator: 100 mg 10/20** **Placebo: 10/20**

* FVFP = First Visit First Patient

Appendix B

Development Core Safety Information or Safety Sections of Investigator Brochure (IB) Available at the Beginning of the Review Period

Version number:

Version date:

Date of last updated version during review period:

Latest version number:

Appendix C

Line Listing

The example below is patterned after the standard line listing originally proposed in the 1992 CIOMS II report (PSURs). In the present context, it should include only SUSARs and suspected unlisted adverse reactions of special interest that were reported during the period for the DSUR, i.e., interval data. Allowance is made for cases that might have both serious and special interest terms (see footnotes to the table).

Company Case Reference Number	Country	Study Code (protocol)	Age (years)	Sex	Total Daily Dose & Route	Treatment Duration (days)	Serious	Drug Relationship	MedDRA Preferred Term* †	Outcome #	Comment
MedDRA SOC											
SOC 1											
SOC 2											
SOC 3											

Serious (Y – yes; N – no; U – unknown)
Drug Relationship (Y – yes; N – no; U – unknown)
* = SUSAR term
† = ADR of Special Interest
# = 1 – recovered; 2 – recovered with sequelae; 3 – not recovered; 4 – recovering; 5 – fatal; 6 – unknown

Appendix D

Cumulative Summary Tabulation*

SOC	Event (PT or HGLT)	Com-parator	Placebo	Study Drug	Blind Treat-ment	Total
SOC 1	Adverse event 13	4	2	1		7
	Adverse event 5			1	72	73
	Adverse event 6	2	1	2		5
	Adverse event 7		1	5		6
SOC 1 Total		6	4	9	72	91
SOC 2	Adverse event 1	7	4	8		19
	Adverse event 2				35	35
	Adverse event 3	4	2	8	7	21
	Adverse event 4			1	38	39
SOC 2 Total		11	6	17	80	114
TOTAL		**17**	**10**	**26**	**152**	**205**

* Due to the interim nature of these data, this tabulation may include data from ongoing clinical trials which may not have been reconciled.

Appendix E

Summary Tabulations by Selected Parameters

Summary Tabulation by Indication*

		Indication 1					Indication 2					
SOC	Event (PT or HGLT)	Comparator	Placebo	Study Drug	Blind Treatment	Indication 1 Total	Comparator	Placebo	Study Drug	Blind Treatment	Indication 2 Total	Total
SOC 1	Adverse event 13		1	1		2	4	1			5	7
	Adverse event 5			1	46	47				26	26	73
	Adverse event 6	2	1	1		4			1		1	5
	Adverse event 7			5		5		1			1	6
SOC 1 Total		2	2	8	46	58	4	2	1	26	33	91
SOC 2	Adverse event 1	6	2	5		13	1	2	3		6	19
	Adverse event 2				7	7				28	28	35
	Adverse event 3		1	5	7	13	4	1	3		8	21
	Adverse event 4			1	21	22				17	17	39
SOC 2 Total		6	3	11	35	55	5	3	6	45	59	114
TOTAL		**8**	**5**	**19**	**81**	**113**	**9**	**5**	**7**	**71**	**92**	**205**

* Due to the interim nature of these data, this tabulation may include data from ongoing clinical trials which may not have been reconciled.

Summary Tabulation by Age Group*

		Adult					Child					
SOC	Event (PT or HGLT)	Comparator	Placebo	Study Drug	Blind Treatment	Adult Total	Comparator	Placebo	Study Drug	Blind Treatment	Child Total	Total
SOC 1	Adverse event 13	4	1	1		6		1			1	7
	Adverse event 5			1	29	30				43	43	73
	Adverse event 6		1			1	2		2		4	5
	Adverse event 7			5		5		1			1	6
SOC 1 Total		4	2	7	29	42	2	2	2	43	49	91
SOC 2	Adverse event 1	1	2	4		7	6	2	4		12	19
	Adverse event 2				5	5				30	30	35
	Adverse event 3	4	1	5		10		1	3	7	11	21
	Adverse event 4				29	29			1	9	10	39
SOC 2 Total		5	3	9	34	51	6	3	8	46	63	114
TOTAL		**9**	**5**	**16**	**63**	**93**	**8**	**5**	**10**	**89**	**112**	**205**

* Due to the interim nature of these data, this tabulation may include data from ongoing clinical trials which may not have been reconciled.

Summary Tabulation for Study "CCC" in which Both Children and Adults are Recruited for Hypertension*

		Adult				Child		
SOC	Event (PT or HGLT)	Comparator	Study Drug	Blind Treatment	Adult Total	Blind Treatment	Child Total	Total
SOC 1	Adverse event 5	4			4			4
	Adverse event 13			8	8			8
SOC 1 Total		4		8	12			12
SOC 2	Adverse event 1	1	2		3			3
	Adverse event 2					15	15	15
	Adverse event 3	4			4			4
	Adverse event 4			8	8	8	8	16
SOC 2 Total		5	2	8	15	23	23	38
TOTAL		**9**	**2**	**16**	**27**	**23**	**23**	**50**

* Due to the interim nature of these data, this tabulation may include data from ongoing clinical trials which may not have been reconciled.

IV

Integrating Pre-Approval (DSUR) With Post-Approval (PSUR) Safety Reporting

Influenced by long-standing practice and current regulatory requirements in several countries and regions, the CIOMS VII Working Group has proposed in this report a harmonized Development Safety Update Report (DSUR) for use during drug development and generally during the conduct of clinical trial programmes. It is the hope of this Working Group that the DSUR will enhance the efficiency and utility of pre-approval safety reporting.

However, as pointed out in Chapter I (section b.), the Working Group believes that this model for periodic safety reporting could be further enhanced. Specifically, the Working Group believes that integration of the DSUR with the PSUR would provide a more efficient method to assemble and convey important safety information to relevant stakeholders, and could provide more complete and consistent information. Therefore, looking to the future, the Working Group considered ways to align the DSUR with the PSUR as closely as possible. The rationale is articulated below:

- Acquisition and assessment of safety data are continuous processes starting with the first exposure of humans during the first Phase I study, maintained throughout the development process, and continuing throughout the marketed use of the product. Although the types of data sources and their relative importance may change during the life cycle of the product (e.g., from pre-approval clinical trials to spontaneous reporting and other sources), safety evaluation is a continuum that evolves with product use and patient exposure.

- While a new drug is still under development in some countries, it might already be on the market in others, where Phase 4 studies may be conducted according to local labelling (official product information). In such situations, under current regulations, sponsors may be required to prepare both an annual report on clinical trials and a PSUR to satisfy the local regulatory requirements. However, the reports may overlap considerably in the types of information included, since the PSUR is expected to contain relevant safety information from, among other sources, clinical trials wherever they may be conducted. Similarly, the DSUR would be expected to contain important information arising from market use of the product, including data from Phase 4 studies.

- Administrative information concerning the regulatory status of authorised products can be relevant to the assessment of safety, not only after marketing authorisation (PSUR), but also prior to marketing authorisation (DSUR).

- Recently approved products commonly undergo continued development for additional uses (indications, dosage forms, populations), necessitating the creation of DSURs, possibly for many years. Meanwhile, PSURs would also be required, giving rise to unnecessary overlap, as mentioned above.

After extensive discussion and debate, CIOMS Working Group VII came to the conclusion that a new perspective is needed for a logical and sequential process that would ensure optimal presentation of periodic safety information to provide an overall safety view, no matter the stage of development or marketing. The Working Group sought a way to make this process efficient, in order to ensure that relevant information is provided to appropriate parties without duplication or confusion. The Working Group recognises that the PSUR as defined under ICH E2C and ICH E2C Addendum is now a well-established document required or recommended by many regulatory authorities. However, the Working Group believes that with minor modifications to its outline, it would be possible to create a single periodic report that would encompass all the information necessary for both product development and post-marketing situations. Naturally, until a product gains initial approval, sections of such an integrated report that deal with marketing experience would remain empty. However, the objective is to take advantage of the well-established PSUR structure and practice with an aim to: 1) convey all pertinent data to all recipients, whether the drug has been approved or is only in development; and 2) to simplify the transition from a "pure" DSUR situation (no approval anywhere in the world) to one in which a PSUR is required.

The Working Group is not proposing any major changes to the basic format or content of the currently used PSUR. Rather, we are introducing for consideration a way to incorporate sections or sub-sections within the PSUR structure that pertain to data accumulated during clinical development, sections that would not ordinarily be presented in a PSUR. Such a structure would allow for selective review of the document when, for example, different personnel within a regulatory body have responsibilities for pre- and post-approval periods.

In practice, if the DSUR proposal of the CIOMS VII Working Group is adopted, commercial sponsors would experience three situations for periodic reporting under the current regulatory framework:

(1) A "pure" DSUR situation would occur for products that have not gained marketing authorisation (or might never do so). The report

would cover only the results of pre-approval clinical trials (and other information, such as pertinent non-clinical and product quality/manufacturing data). Thus, there would be no post-approval data of any kind included for the investigational product.[1, 2]

(2) A DSUR/PSUR situation would occur: (a) for products approved for marketing in one or more locations while still unapproved and under investigation in others; and (b) for approved products that are under investigation for a new use (indication, dosage form, or population).

(3) A "pure" PSUR situation would occur when all Phase I – III activity had been completed, and the only information available would come from marketed use or post-approval studies (e.g., Phase IV and observational studies).

Most often, non-commercial sponsors of clinical trials (institutions, academic centres, independent investigators) would probably be subject to situation 1, since their responsibilities typically involve specific clinical trials. However, they may also study new uses of approved products independent of a commercial sponsor (situation 2).

Some technical difficulties currently arise in trying to reconcile the DSUR with the PSUR. For example, the PSUR has an International Birth Date (IBD) representing the date of first marketing approval anywhere in the world. However, as proposed for the DSUR, its starting point is the Development IBD (DIBD), the date of first approval anywhere to conduct one or more clinical trials with the product. This particular lack of synchrony is discussed in Chapter II.a.(6), and the Working Group provides a recommendation, at least for the situation when separate DSURs and PSURs are prepared. Whether that proposal would be the most suitable solution for an integrated DSUR-PSUR model remains to be considered.

Another key issue relates to the periodicity of reporting, which is not necessarily the same under the proposed requirements for a DSUR (annually) and PSUR (six-monthly, annually, and other periodicity). With an integrated DSUR-PSUR report, there may still be a need for different

---

1 If there were relevant data on a marketed product in the same class as the investigational drug, they would be included.

2 The Working Group notes that some development programmes are discontinued prior to any attempts to obtain marketing approval (for safety, efficacy or other reasons), or a marketing application at the end of a development programme may not be approved by any regulatory authority. In such situations, there will never be the need for a PSUR.

periodicities, especially when a product is in its early stages of development in some locations but on the market in others.

In countries or regions where non-commercial sponsors are not required to submit PSURs (e.g., the EU), then an alternative DSUR-only format and content could be used to simplify their reporting.

These and other issues remain unresolved. It is worth noting that there is extensive similarity and consistency between the currently required format and content of the PSUR and the newly proposed DSUR, the latter by design to align the two as closely as possible. A comparison is shown in Appendix 6. With that in mind, Appendix 7 contains an example of how a Table of Contents might appear for an integrated report.

However, the format and content for an integrated DSUR-PSUR report will have to be the subject of a separate initiative, perhaps under CIOMS. Therefore, the sample Table of Contents should be considered only a starting point for future consideration of the principles and practices underlying such a report, and to stimulate discussion.

Appendix 1

Procedure and Membership of CIOMS Working Group VII

CIOMS Working Group VI, in its 2005 published report, "Management of Safety Information from Clinical Trials" (CIOMS, Geneva, 2005), noted that there are differences in the regulatory requirements as to how clinical trial sponsors should submit periodic safety reports from new drug developmental research prior to submission for a marketing authorisation. The Working Group recommended the development of a new, harmonised annual safety report for regulators and asked the CIOMS Secretariat to draft an outline for a Development Safety Update Report (DSUR) that would replace current reports.

The draft outline of the DSUR was the subject of consultations in November-December 2004 among the regulatory and industry scientist members of CIOMS WG VI, who suggested that CIOMS should establish a Working Group to prepare details of the format, content and timing of such a report.

CIOMS Working Group VII on the Development Safety Update Report (DSUR) was established in January 2005 and met for the first time at Heathrow Airport, UK in March 2005. The Working Group met four times subsequently: in Washington DC, USA in June 2005, in Koenigstein, Germany in October 2005, in New York City, USA in January 2006, and in Paris, France in March 2006. Individual topic chapters and other sections for drafting guidance on the DSUR were assigned to subgroups in the project. The draft texts and concepts were subsequently reviewed, discussed and debated several times within the entire Working Group, which led to revisions and refinements of the texts.

Members of the Working Group took turns at chairing the meetings and L. Hostelley served as secretary of the project.

A. J. Gordon, L. Hostelley, L. Hunt, F. Maignen, H. Mickail, V. Simmons, and E. Unger formed the Editorial Group, with part-time assistance by M. Ward. The Editorial Group met in person or via teleconference on several occasions from March through August 2006. E. Unger compiled the late-stage draft consolidated texts, and A. J. Gordon and E. Unger prepared and edited the final manuscript for publication by CIOMS.

Listed below are 24 senior scientists from drug regulatory authorities and pharmaceutical companies, including three consultants who participated in the project.

Name	Organization	Part-time/full-time
Maureen Caulfield	Wyeth	Full-time
Gaby Danan	sanofi-aventis	Full-time
Paul Dolin	F. Hoffmann-LaRoche	Part-time
Reinhard Fescharek	Bayer HealthCare AG	Full-time
E. Stewart Geary	Eisai Co., Ltd.	Full-time
Trevor G. Gibbs	GlaxoSmithKline	Full-time
Arnold J. Gordon	Consultant	Full-time
Linda S. Hostelley	Merck & Co., Inc.	Full-time
Martin Huber	F. Hoffmann-LaRoche	Part-time
Leonie Hunt	Therapeutic Good Administration (TGA, Australia)	Full-time
Juhana E. Idänpään-Heikkilä	CIOMS	Full-time
Gottfried Kreutz	BfArM and BMG (Germany)	Full-time
François Maignen	EMEA (EU)	Full-time
Hani Mickail	Novartis	Full-time
Siddika Mithani	Health Canada	Full-time
Claudio Nava	Pfizer Inc.	Full-time
Junko Sato	Pharmaceuticals and Medical Devices Agency (Japan)	Full-time
Valerie Simmons	Eli Lilly and Company	Full-time
Wendy Stephenson	Consultant	Part-time
Akiyoshi Uchiyama	Artage, Inc.	Full-time
Ellis Unger	FDA (USA)	Full-time
Valerie Vandevoorde	Pfizer Inc.	Full-time
Philippe Vella	AFSSAPS (France)	Full-time
Martyn Ward	MHRA (UK)	Full-time

Appendix 2

Glossary

This glossary contains key terms used in this report and those considered necessary to interpret the Working Group's recommendations. Several of the terms are in common use and are variably defined in various forums, having specific regional and local meanings. Whenever possible the Working Group has adopted terminology and definitions in use in ICH guidelines or those previously proposed by CIOMS Working Groups, recognising the importance of these two bodies in harmonisation activities for improving the regulatory outcome. In particular, the Glossary from the report of the CIOMS VI Working Group (Management of Safety Information from Clinical Trials, CIOMS, Geneva 2005) has been one of the main sources for development of this Glossary.

For some terms, definitions used in the EU have been included in recognition of relatively recent regulatory requirements. However, this should not be seen as an endorsement by the Working Group of any particular definitions over those of other regions, and the Working Group is supportive of any efforts to agree on internationally harmonised terms.

For more detailed discussion of the terminology and of matters surrounding the conduct of clinical trials, readers are referred to ICH guidelines and previous CIOMS Working Group reports. Definitions used in some jurisdictions may be derived from WHO sources, and this is an important additional potential resource.

Unless otherwise specified, definitions are taken from ICH Guidelines and from *Management of Safety Information from Clinical Trials,* Report of CIOMS Working Group VI.

Adverse Drug Reaction

In the pre-approval clinical experience with a new medicinal product or its new usages, particularly when the therapeutic dose(s) may not be established: All noxious and unintended responses to a medicinal product related to any dose should be considered adverse drug reactions. The phrase "responses to a medicinal product" means that a causal relationship between a

medicinal product and an adverse event is at least a reasonable possibility, i.e., the relationship cannot be ruled out.
Source: ICH Guideline for Good Clinical Practice E6(R1)

> *In the EU Directive 2001/20/EC on Clinical trials: "Adverse Reaction: – all untoward and unintended responses to an investigational medicinal product related to any dose administered."*
>
> *Commentary: As shown, the current ICH definition includes the phrase "i.e., the relationship cannot be ruled out." The CIOMS Working Group believes that it is virtually impossible to rule out with any certainty the role of the drug on the basis of a single case. Therefore, we recommend elimination of that phrase and prefer the ICH E2A elaboration of "reasonable possibility" to mean that there are facts, evidence, or arguments to support a causal association with the drug.*

Adverse Event/Adverse Experience

Any untoward medical occurrence in a patient or clinical investigation subject administered a pharmaceutical product and which does not necessarily have a causal relationship with this treatment. An adverse event (AE) can therefore be any unfavourable and unintended sign (including an abnormal laboratory finding), symptom, or disease temporally associated with the use of a medicinal (investigational) product, whether or not related to the medicinal (investigational) product.
Source: ICH Guideline for Good Clinical Practice E6(R1)

> *In the EU Directive 2001/20/EC on Clinical trials: "Adverse Event:" any untoward medical occurrence in a patient or clinical trial subject administered a medicinal product and which does not necessarily have a causal relationship with this treatment.*

Adverse Event of Special Interest

An adverse event of special interest (serious or non-serious) is one of scientific and medical concern specific to the sponsor's product or programme, for which ongoing monitoring and rapid communication by the investigator to the sponsor may be appropriate. Such an event may require further investigation in order to characterize and understand it. Depending on the nature of the event, rapid communication by the trial sponsor to other parties may also be needed (e.g., regulators).
Source: Proposed by the CIOMS VI Working Group

Commentary: An adverse event of special interest is a noteworthy event for the particular product or class of products that a sponsor may wish to monitor carefully. It could be serious or non-serious (e.g., hair loss, loss of taste, impotence), and could include events that might be potential precursors or prodromes for more serious medical conditions in susceptible individuals. Such events should be described in protocols or protocol amendments, and instruction provided for investigators as to how and when they should be reported to the sponsor.

Clinical Trial/Clinical Study

Any investigation in human subjects intended to discover or verify the clinical, pharmacological and/or other pharmacodynamic effects of an investigational product(s), and/or to identify any adverse reactions to an investigational product(s), and/or to study absorption, distribution, metabolism, and excretion of an investigational product(s) with the object of ascertaining its safety and/or efficacy. The terms "clinical trial" and "clinical study" are synonymous.
Source: ICH E6 Guideline (GCP)

Company Core Safety Information (CCSI)

All relevant safety information contained in the Company Core Data Sheet prepared by the MAH (Marketing Authorisation Holder) and which the MAH requires to be listed in all countries where the company markets the drug, except when the local regulatory authority specifically requires a modification. It is the reference information by which listed and unlisted are determined for the purpose of periodic reporting for marketed products, but not by which expected and unexpected are determined for expedited reporting.
Source: ICH Guideline E2C: Periodic Safety Update Report of Marketed Drugs

Commentary: The CIOMS VI Working Group suggested that for drugs on the market in some places while under investigation in others, consideration should be given to using the CCSI as the basis for expedited reporting on cases arising in post-approval (Phase 4) clinical trials. See Chapter 7, section b.(3). of the CIOMS VI report.

Compassionate Use

The use of an unapproved drug in an individual patient with a serious medical condition where the use of an unproven therapy is justified due to the lack of alternative safe and effective treatments.
Source: Proposed by CIOMS Working Group VII

> *Commentary: Some medical dictionaries define "compassionate use" as a method of providing experimental therapeutics prior to final regulatory approval for use in humans. This procedure is often used with very sick individuals who have no other treatment options. Often, case-by-case approval must be obtained from the regulatory authority for "compassionate use" of a drug or other therapy.*

Completed Clinical Trial

Study for which a final clinical study report is available.
Source: Proposed by CIOMS Working Group VII

> *Commentary: As a reminder, ICH Guideline E3 (Structure and content of clinical study reports) is the template for final study reports in use by most commercial sponsors.*

Data Lock Point for DSUR

The date (month and day) designated as the annual cut-off for data to be included in a DSUR. It is based on the Development International Birth Date (DIBD).
Source: Proposed by CIOMS Working Group VII

Development Core Safety Information (DCSI)

An independent section of an Investigator's Brochure (IB) identical in structure to the Company Core Safety Information (CCSI) that contains a summary of all relevant safety information that is described in more detail within the main body of the IB. It is the reference safety document that determines whether an ADR is listed or unlisted.
Source: Guidelines for Preparing Core Clinical Safety Information on Drugs. Second Edition. Report of CIOMS Working Groups III and V, CIOMS, Geneva, 1999

Development International Birth Date (DIBD)

Date of first approval (or authorisation) for conducting an interventional clinical trial in any country.
Source: Proposed by CIOMS Working Group VII

Development Pharmacovigilance and Risk Management Plan (DPRMP) or Development Risk Management Plan (DRMP)

A plan to conduct activities relating to the detection, assessment, understanding, reporting and prevention of adverse effects of medicines during clinical trials. This plan should be initiated early and modified as necessary throughout the development process for a new drug or drug-use.
Source: This term and definition were proposed by CIOMS Working Group VI

Development Safety Update Report (DSUR)

A periodic summary of safety information for regulators, including benefit-risk considerations, for a drug, biologic or vaccine under development or study, prepared by the sponsor of the clinical trial(s).
Source: Based on the term and definition originally proposed by CIOMS Working Group VI

> *Commentary: A DSUR should serve as a summary of the safety experience in all clinical trials for a drug in development, including trials for new uses of an already approved drug (e.g., new dosage forms, indications, populations). In practice, it can serve as the foundation for any changes in the Investigator's Brochure and /or Development Core Safety Information (DCSI). The benefit-risk relationship mentioned in this definition does not refer to the traditional concept covering the product itself; rather, it refers to the ongoing estimation as to whether the subjects or patients are well served by continuing in a clinical trial or development programme. See Chapter I, Section c. for more discussion.*

Expected and Unexpected Adverse Drug Reaction (See also Listed and Unlisted)

An expected ADR is one for which its nature or severity is consistent with that included in the appropriate reference safety information (e.g., Investigator's Brochure for an unapproved investigational drug or package insert/summary of product characteristics for an approved product).

An unexpected ADR is defined as: An adverse reaction, the nature or severity of which is not consistent with the applicable product information (e.g., Investigator's Brochure for an unapproved investigational drug or package insert/summary of product characteristics for an approved product).
Source: Current Challenges in Pharmacovigilance: Pragmatic Approaches, Report of CIOMS Working Group V, CIOMS, Geneva, 2001, p. 109; ICH Guideline for Good Clinical Practice E6(R1)
Note: ICH does not define "expected adverse drug reaction."

> *In the EU: "Unexpected Adverse Reaction" – an adverse reaction, the nature or severity of which is not consistent with the applicable product information (e.g., investigator's brochure for an unauthorised investigational drug or summary of product characteristics for an authorised product).*
>
> *Commentary: The concept of "expectedness" refers to events which may or may not have been previously observed and documented. It does not refer to what might have been anticipated (expected in a different sense) from the known pharmacological properties of the active substance.*

Identified risk

An untoward occurrence for which there is adequate evidence of an association with the medicinal product of interest. Examples of identified risks include:

- an adverse reaction adequately demonstrated in non-clinical studies and confirmed by clinical data
- an adverse reaction observed in well designed clinical trials or epidemiological studies for which the magnitude of the difference compared with the comparator group (placebo or active substance) on a parameter of interest suggests a causal relationship
- an adverse reaction suggested by a number of well documented spontaneous reports where causality is strongly supported by temporal relationship and biological plausibility, such as anaphylactic reactions or application site reactions.

Source: Guideline on Risk Management Systems for Medicinal Products for Human Use (EMEA/CHMP/96268/2005)

Important Identified Risk, Important Potential Risk or Important Missing Information

An identified risk, potential risk, or missing information that could impact on the risk-benefit balance of the product or have implications for public health.
Source: Guideline on Risk Management Systems for Medicinal Products for Human Use (EMEA/CHMP/96268/2005)

Independent Data-Monitoring Committee (IDMC), Data and Safety Monitoring Board (DSMB), Monitoring Committee, Data Monitoring Committee (DMC)

An independent data-monitoring committee that may be established by the sponsor to assess, at intervals, the progress of a clinical trial, the safety data, and the critical efficacy endpoints, and to recommend to the sponsor whether to continue, modify, or stop a trial.
Source: ICH Guideline for Good Clinical Practice E6(R1)

> *Commentary: Data monitoring committees/boards are referred to by several names and they may have different roles and responsibilities depending on the particular circumstances. For convenience and consistency, the CIOMS Working Group favours the term Data and Safety Monitoring Board (DSMB). DSMBs are responsible for monitoring and reviewing both safety and efficacy data, not just "critical study endpoints." For detailed discussion on DSMBs, see the Report of CIOMS Working Group VI, specifically Appendix 5 and the references in Chapter II, section b.*

Independent Ethics Committee (IEC) (See also "Institutional Review Board")

An independent body (a review board or a committee, institutional, regional, national, or supranational), constituted of medical/scientific professionals and non-medical/non-scientific members, whose responsibility it is to ensure the protection of the rights, safety, and well-being of human subjects involved in the trial and to provide public assurance of that protection, by, among other things, reviewing and approving/providing favourable opinion on, the trial protocol, the suitability of the investigator(s), facilities, and the methods and material to be used in obtaining and documenting informed consent of the trial subjects.

The legal status, composition, function, operations and regulatory requirements pertaining to Independent Ethics Committees may differ among countries, but should allow the Independent Ethics Committee to act in agreement with GCP as described in the ICH Guideline for Good Clinical Practice E6(R1).
Source: ICH Guideline for Good Clinical Practice E6(R1)

> *In the EU Directive 2001/20/EC on Clinical trials: "Ethics Committee" – an independent body in a Member State, consisting of healthcare professionals and non-medical members, whose responsibility it is to protect the rights, safety and well being of human subjects involved in a trial and to provide public assurance of that protection, by among other things, expressing an opinion on the trial protocol, the suitability of the investigators and the adequacy of facilities, and on the methods and documents to be used to inform trial subjects and obtain their informed consent.*

Institutional Review Board (IRB)
(See also "Independent Ethics Committee")

An independent body constituted of medical, scientific, and non-scientific members, whose responsibility is to ensure the protection of the rights, safety and well-being of human subjects involved in the trial by, among other things, reviewing, approving, and providing continuing review of trial protocol and amendments and of the methods and material to be used in obtaining and documenting informed consent of the trial subjects.
Source: ICH Guideline for Good Clinical Practice E6(R1)

> *Commentary: IEC and IRB are generally used synonymously. However, depending on country or region, the term IRB may be used instead of IEC (or EC), especially if the term is specified in regulations or may be legally binding (e.g., IRB in the U.S). There also may be slight differences between Ethics Committees and Institutional Review Boards. For detailed discussion, see Chapter II of the Report of CIOMS Working Group VI.*

Interventional Clinical Trial
(See also "Non-Interventional Clinical Trial")

An interventional clinical trial is any research study that prospectively assigns people to one or more health-related interventions (e.g., preventive

care, drugs, surgical procedures, behavioural treatments, etc.) to evaluate their effects on health-related outcomes.
Source: WHO International Clinical Trials Registry Platform (ICTRP) (http://www.who.int/ictrp/glossary/en/index.html)

Investigational Drug

The term "investigational drug" is used to refer to the product that is the object of experiment, whether it is a drug, biologic or vaccine.
Source: Proposed by CIOMS Working Group VII

> *Commentary: This term is chosen to distinguish it from the term "Investigational Medicinal Product," which refers in some regulatory settings (e.g., EU) to all the treatments used in a trial: placebo, active comparators or the "experimental" product.*

Labelled or Unlabelled (See also "Expected" and "Unexpected")

For a product with an approved marketing application, any reaction which is not mentioned in the official product information is "unlabelled." If it is included it is termed "labelled."
Source: Current Challenges in Pharmacovigilance: Report of CIOMS Working Group V, CIOMS, Geneva, 2001

Listed/Unlisted

Any reaction which is not included in the Development Company Core Safety Information within a company's core data sheet for an investigational or developmental product is "unlisted." If it is included it is termed "listed."
Source: Proposed by CIOMS Working Groups III and V

> *Commentary: The terms "listed" and "unlisted" were purposely adopted in ICH Guideline E2C (Periodic Safety Update Reports for Marketed Drugs) for use with internal company safety information documents, so as to distinguish them from the terms labelled and unlabelled, which should only be used in association with official "labelling," i.e., the SPC or Package Insert, and generally the regulator-approved data sheets for marketed products. The usage of listed/unlisted has been extended to the Development Core Safety Information (DCSI) as recommended in* Guideline for Preparing Core Clinical-Safety Information on Drugs, *Second Edition, CIOMS Working Group III/V, CIOMS, Geneva, 1999*

MedDRA (Medical Dictionary for Regulatory Activities)

MedDRA is a clinically validated medical terminology for regulatory authorities and the regulated pharmaceutical industry for utilisation in data entry, retrieval, evaluation and presentation, in both pre- and post- marketing phases of the regulatory process. It covers diseases, diagnoses, signs, symptoms, therapeutic indications, investigation names and qualitative results, as well as medical and surgical procedures, medical, social and family history. MedDRA is one of the standards required for the electronic transmission of ICSR (individual case safety reports). Recommendations on the use of MedDRA are set out in an ICH endorsed 'Points to consider' document, as updated from time to time.
Source: ICH Topic M1: Medical Terminology (MedDRA)
For more information see the website www.meddramsso.com/MSSOWeb/.

Missing Information

Information about the safety of a medicinal product which is not available at the time of submission of the Risk Management Plan and which represents a limitation of the safety data with respect to predicting the safety of the product in the marketplace.
Source: Guideline on Risk Management Systems for Medicinal Products for Human Use (EMEA/CHMP/96268/2005)

Multidisciplinary Safety Management Team (SMT)

A team established within a sponsor company, the composition of which will vary over time. The team is responsible for the timely review, assessment and evaluation of incoming safety data.
Source: From the report of CIOMS Working Group VI

Non-Interventional Clinical Trial (See also "Interventional Clinical Trial")

A study where the medicinal product(s) is (are) prescribed in the usual manner in accordance with the terms of the marketing authorisation. The assignment of the patient to a particular therapeutic strategy is not decided in advance by a trial protocol but falls within current practice and the prescription of the medicine is clearly separated from the decision to include the patient in the study. No additional diagnostic or monitoring procedures shall be applied to the patients and epidemiological methods shall be used for the analysis of collected data.

Source: EU Directive 2001/20/EC on Clinical trials and detailed guidance on the collection, verification and presentation of adverse reaction reports arising from clinical trials on medicinal products for human use, ENTR/CT 3 Revision 2 dated April 2006.

> *Commentary: Observational studies (usually retrospective examination and analysis of existing data from medical practice data bases) are often referred to as non-interventional studies.*

Ongoing Clinical Trial

Study where enrolment has begun, whether a hold is in place or analysis is complete, but without a final clinical study report available.
Source: Proposed by CIOMS Working Group VII

Pharmacovigilance

The science and activities relating to the detection, assessment, understanding and prevention of adverse effects or any other drug-related problems.
Source: The Importance of Pharmacovigilance – Safety Monitoring of Medicinal Products, World Health Organization, 2002 (ISBN 92 4159 015 7), and ICH Guideline E2E, Pharmacovigilance Planning.

> *Commentary: There is some uncertainty concerning the phrase "any other drug-related problems." At least in the present context, the CIOMS Working Group VII understands the phrase to refer to issues that could affect the safety and safe use of medicines, such as medication errors and potential product quality issues including quality defects. The CIOMS Working Group VII endorses the use of the term "Pharmacovigilance" for clinical safety activities throughout the lifecycle of a medicinal product.*

PHASES OF CLINICAL STUDIES (I-IV)

Phase I (most typical kind of study: Human Pharmacology)

Initial trials provide an early evaluation of short-term safety and tolerability and can provide pharmacodynamic and pharmacokinetic information needed to choose a suitable dosage range and administration schedule for initial exploratory therapeutic trials.

Phase II (most typical kind of study: Therapeutic Exploratory)

Phase II is usually considered to start with the initiation of studies in which the primary objective is to explore therapeutic efficacy in patients.

Phase III (most typical kind of study: Therapeutic Confirmatory)

Phase III usually is considered to begin with the initiation of studies in which the primary objective is to demonstrate or confirm therapeutic benefit.

Phase IV (variety of studies: Therapeutic Use)

Phase IV begins after drug approval. Therapeutic use studies go beyond the prior demonstration of the drug's safety, efficacy and dose definition. Studies in Phase IV are all studies (other than routine surveillance) performed after drug approval and related to the approved indication. They are studies that were not considered necessary for approval but are often important for optimising the drug's use. They may be of any type but should have valid scientific objectives. Commonly conducted studies include additional drug-drug interaction, dose response or safety studies, and studies designed to support use under the approved indication, e.g., mortality/morbidity studies, epidemiological studies.
Source: ICH Topic E8: General Considerations for Clinical Trials.

Commentary: ICH Guideline E8 has proposed that studies be categorized according to their objectives (human pharmacology, therapeutic exploratory, therapeutic confirmatory, and therapeutic use) as distinct from the traditional concept based strictly on temporal phases of drug development. For example, human pharmacology studies (traditionally referred to as Phase I) can be and often are conducted throughout a product's lifetime (even though they are referred to as "Initial trials..." in the definition given). In some settings, other terms are used to categorize study types; for example, Phase IIA studies are sometimes referred to as "proof of concept studies," Phase IIB can refer to studies that establish proper dosing, and Phase IIIB refers to "peri-approval" studies (Phase IV-like studies initiated prior to drug approval). Depending on the product and nature of the programme, there may not be a sharp or distinct division between the various phases of trials.

The CIOMS Working Group believes that the ICH definition of Phase IV studies needs modification by deleting the expression "(other than routine surveillance)," which is not accurate, and by emphasizing that such studies should be limited to uses and conditions specified within the approved product information (SPC, Package Insert, etc.).

Potential Risk

An untoward occurrence for which there is some basis for suspicion of an association with the medicinal product of interest but where an association has not been confirmed. Examples of potential risk include:

- non-clinical safety concerns that have not been observed or resolved in clinical studies
- adverse events observed in clinical trials or epidemiological studies for which the magnitude of the difference, compared with the comparator group (placebo or active substance) or unexposed group, on the parameter of interest raises a suspicion of, but is not large enough to suggest, a causal relationship
- a signal arising from a spontaneous adverse reaction reporting system
- an event which is known to be associated with other products of the same class or which could be expected to occur based on the properties of the medicinal product.

Source: Guideline on Risk Management Systems for Medicinal Products for Human Use (EMEA/CHMP/96268/2005)

The CIOMS Working Group VII endorses this meaning as applied in this report.

Protocol Related Adverse Event

An adverse event that is thought to be related to an aspect of a procedure or measurement as specified within the clinical trial protocol, but not directly or solely related to the administration of the drug or drugs under investigation.
Source: Proposed by CIOMS Working Group VII

Registry

A registry is a list of patients presenting with the same characteristic(s). This characteristic can be a disease (disease registry) or a specific exposure (drug registry). Both types of registries, which only differ by the type of patient data of interest, can collect a battery of information using standardised questionnaires in a prospective fashion.
Source: ICH Guideline E2E, Pharmacovigilance Planning

Commentary: Exposure (drug) registries address populations exposed to drugs of interest (e.g., a registry of rheumatoid arthritis patients exposed to biological therapies) to determine if a drug has a special impact on this group of patients. Some exposure (drug) registries address drug exposure in specific populations, such as pregnant women; however, pregnancy registries exist without any particular exposure in mind. Patients can be followed over time and included in a cohort study to collect data on adverse events using standardised questionnaires. Single cohort studies can measure incidence, but, without a comparison group, cannot provide proof of association. However, they can be useful for signal amplification, particularly of rare outcomes. This type of registry can be very valuable.

Serious Adverse Event or Reaction

Any untoward medical occurrence that at any dose:

Results in death
Is life-threatening*
Requires in-patient hospitalisation or prolongation of existing hospitalisation
Results in persistent or significant disability/incapacity, or
Is a congenital anomaly/birth defect

Medical and scientific judgement should be exercised in deciding whether expedited reporting is appropriate in other situations, such as important medical events that may not be immediately life-threatening or result in death or hospitalisation but may jeopardise the patient or may require intervention to prevent one of the other outcomes listed in the definition above. *These should usually be considered serious as well.* Examples of such events are intensive treatment in an emergency room or at home for allergic bronchospasm; blood dyscrasias or convulsions that do not result in hospitalisation; or development of drug dependency or drug abuse.

Source: ICH Guideline E2A: Definitions and Standards for Expedited Reporting and ICH Guideline E2D: Post-approval Safety Data Management – Note for Guidance on Definitions and Standards for Expedited Reporting

In the EU Directive 2001/20/EC on Clinical trials: "Serious Adverse Event or Serious Adverse Reaction" – any untoward medical occur-

---

* The term "life-threatening" refers to an event or reaction in which the patient was at risk of death at the time of the event or reaction; it does not refer to an event or reaction which hypothetically might have caused death if it were more severe.

rence or effect that at any dose results in death, is life-threatening, requires hospitalisation or prolongation of existing hospitalisation, results in persistent or significant disability or incapacity, or is a congenital anomaly or birth defect.

Commentary: The ICH definition of a serious AE or ADR has been adopted for post marketing applications in ICH Guideline E2D. The EU definition given above is considered by the CIOMS Working Group as incomplete without the paragraph beginning with "Medical and scientific judgement..." in the ICH definition.

Signal

A report or reports of an event with an unknown causal relationship to treatment that is recognised as worthy of further exploration and continued surveillance.
Source: Benefit-Risk Balance for Marketed Drugs. Report of CIOMS Working Group IV, CIOMS, Geneva, 1998; and Dictionary of Pharmacoepidemiology, by B. Bégaud, John Wiley & Sons, Ltd., Hoboken, USA, 2000

Commentary: A signal can arise from non-clinical as well as clinical sources. It should be based on data and not theory, and can refer not only to a new (unexpected) and potentially important event, but also to an unexpected finding for an already known event, such as information on an ADR related to the nature (specificity), intensity, rate of occurrence or other clinically relevant finding that represents a meaningful change from that expected in the subject/patient population under investigation or treatment. A signal is not a confirmed finding, but is generally referred to as an hypothesis-generating situation that must be validated ("signal strengthening") or disproved.

An older definition of a signal by the WHO Collaborating Centre for International Drug Monitoring (BMJ, 304:465, 22 February 1992) focused on post-marketing conditions and predated the new definitions of adverse event and adverse reaction introduced under ICH: "Reported information on a possible causal relationship between an adverse event and a drug, the relationship being unknown or incompletely documented previously. Usually more than a single report is required to generate a signal, depending upon the seriousness of the event and the quality of the information."

Sponsor

An individual, company, institution, or organization that takes responsibility for the initiation, management, and/or financing of a clinical trial.
Source: ICH Guideline for Good Clinical Practice E6(R1)

SUSAR (Suspected Unexpected Serious Adverse Reactions)

This term and acronym come from an EU Clinical trial Directive Guidance on expedited reporting: "All suspected adverse reactions related to an IMP (the tested IMP and comparators) which occur in the concerned trial that are both unexpected and serious (SUSARs) are subject to expedited reporting." [Note: IMP = investigational medicinal product]
Source: EU Directive 2001/20/EC on Clinical Trials (Article 17). Detailed guidance on the collection, verification and presentation of adverse reports arising from clinical trials on medicinal products for human use, April 2006. ENTR/CT 3 Revision 2.

See also, Detailed guidance on the European Database of Suspected Unexpected Serious Adverse Reactions (EudraVigilance – Clinical Trial Module. ENTR/CT 4. Revision 1).

Appendix 3

US versus EU Annual Safety Reporting Requirements for Investigational Drugs

	US IND Annual Report (21 CFR 312.33)	EU Clinical Trial Directive Annual Safety Reports and accompanying guidance (Directive 2001/20/EC; ENTR/CT3)
ADMINISTRATIVE MATTERS		
Data lock point	Effective date of IND	Date of the first authorisation of a clinical trial of an investigational drug by a competent authority in any Member State (first EUDRACT number before approval; IBD after approval)
Periodicity	Annual	Annual or on request. Prepare one annual safety report for all clinical trials of an investigational drug being tested in any Member State
Recipients	FDA	Member States, Ethics Committees
Purpose	Progress report for clinical trials	Concise safety evaluation and benefit-risk evaluation for the concerned clinical trial
Submission deadline	Within 60 days of data lock point	Within 60 days of data lock point
Short term trials (e.g., Phase I)	For all trials, an end of study report within one year of completion of the study	Within 90 days of the end of trial, submit safety report which contains at least line listings, and if appropriate, aggregate summary tabulations and a statement of the patients' safety experience
Feedback by regulators	On request of sponsor	Not specified

	US IND Annual Report (21 CFR 312.33)	EU Clinical Trial Directive Annual Safety Reports and accompanying guidance (Directive 2001/20/EC; ENTR/CT3)
CONTENT AND FORMAT		
Adverse Experiences Included	All serious including: – serious-associated-expected – serious-associated-unexpected – serious- not associated-expected – serious- not associated-unexpected	Only serious-associated including: – serious-associated-expected – serious-associated-unexpected
Serious Criteria	Death, life-threatening, hospitalisation or prolongation of hospitalisation, persistent or significant disability or incapacity, congenital anomaly or birth defect, and other medical events that may jeopardize the subject or require intervention to prevent serious outcomes	Death, life-threatening, hospitalisation or prolongation of hospitalisation, persistent or significant disability or incapacity, congenital anomaly or birth defect, and other medical events that may jeopardize the subject or require intervention to prevent serious outcomes
Association	Reasonable possibility that the adverse experience may have been caused by study product	Adverse events judged by either the reporting investigator or the sponsor as having a "reasonable causal relationship" (i.e., in general there is evidence or argument to suggest a causal relationship) to a drug
Expectedness	According to investigator brochure (use US package circular (Package Insert) after marketing approval unless study is for a new indication)	According to the reference document as defined in the study protocol: – investigator's brochure for an unapproved investigational drug – summary of product characteristics (SPC) for an authorised drug in the EU which is being used according to the terms and conditions of the marketing authorisation.

	US IND Annual Report (21 CFR 312.33)	EU Clinical Trial Directive Annual Safety Reports and accompanying guidance (Directive 2001/20/EC; ENTR/CT3)
Specific Report Content	**Individual study information:** A summary of the status of each study in progress or completed during the previous year including study title, protocol number, purpose, patient population. For each study provide the total numbers of subjects initially planned for inclusion, entered to date (tabulated by age, gender, race), completed study as planned, and dropouts. If the study has been completed, or if interim results are known, a brief description of any available study results. **Summary information:** A narrative or tabular summary showing the most frequent and most serious adverse experiences by body system. A summary of all IND safety reports (7 and 15 day expedited reports) submitted during the past year. A list of subjects who died during participation in the investigation, with the cause of death for each subject. A list of subjects who dropped out during the course of the investigation in association with any adverse experience, whether or not thought to be drug related. A brief description of what, if anything, was obtained that is pertinent to an understanding of the drug's actions, including, for example, information about dose response, information from controlled trials, and information about bioavailability.	**Report on the subjects' safety in the concerned clinical trial:** A global analysis on the subjects' safety in the concerned clinical trial based on the experience from all clinical trials of the investigational drug. If the sponsor conducts several clinical trials with the same tested investigational drug, the annual safety report should include a concise global analysis of the actual safety profile of the tested investigational drug, based on the experience from all clinical trials performed by the sponsor and all available data. The report should include: – A concise safety analysis, a benefit-risk evaluation, and a description and critical analysis of all new safety findings related to the investigational drug. – An analysis of the implications for the clinical trial population and the safety profile of the investigational drug, taking into account data such as dose, duration, treatment time course, reversibility, evidence of previously unidentified toxicity, increased frequency of toxicity, overdose and its treatment, interactions or other risks factors, special populations, at risk groups, pregnancy or lactation, abuse, investigational or diagnostic procedural risks of the clinical trial. – Supporting results of non-clinical studies or other experiences that are likely to affect the subjects' safety. – Details of measures proposed to minimize risks.

	US IND Annual Report (21 CFR 312.33)	EU Clinical Trial Directive Annual Safety Reports and accompanying guidance (Directive 2001/20/EC; ENTR/CT3)
Specific Report Content	A list of the preclinical studies (including animal studies) completed or in progress during the past year and a summary of the major preclinical findings.	
	A summary of any significant manufacturing or microbiological changes made during the past year. **Other:** A description of the general investigational plan for the coming year. A description of investigator brochure revisions and a copy of the new brochure. A description of any significant Phase I protocol modifications made during the previous year and not previously reported to the IND in a protocol amendment. A summary of significant foreign marketing developments with the drug during the past year (approvals, withdrawals, suspension from marketing). A log of any outstanding IND business for which the sponsor requests or expects a reply, comment, or meeting.	– Rationale for updating the protocol, consent form, patient information leaflet or the investigator's brochure
Line listings of case reports	See above under Specific Report Content: Summary Information	Trial-specific line listing of all reports of serious-associated AEs with separate listings for each treatment arm (investigational drug, comparator, placebo, blinded treatment)
Summary tabulations of AE/ADR terms	See above under Specific Report Content: Summary Information	Aggregate summary tabulations of serious-associated AEs across all concerned trials specifying the numbers of reports for each ADR term and each body system, for each treatment arm (investigational drug, comparator, placebo, blinded treatment), with unexpected ADR terms identified

Appendix 4

This Appendix contains two fictitious, sample DSURs, the first (Appendix 4A) representing the fourth annual DSUR by a pharmaceutical company for a product under development, and the second (Appendix 4B) for an independent investigator-sponsor who is conducting a clinical trial. Both examples follow the principles given in Chapter II and the detailed format and content described in Chapter III. Both examples are fictitious; any resemblance to real products or actual data is unintentional.

A. Sample DSUR for a Commercial Sponsor

CONFIDENTIAL
DEVELOPMENTAL SAFETY UPDATE REPORT

INN	qweasytrol (hydrochloride dihydrate)
Code Name	AR-708
Chemical Name	1,2,3-trimethyl-qweasy
Formulations	Tablet, Intravenous Injection
Reporting Period:	14-Jul-2005 to 13-Jul-2006
Development International Birth Date	14-Jul-2002
DSUR Number	4
Sponsor	Andson Research Ltd. 61157 Healey Square London N1 2NW, UK

This Developmental Safety Update Report contains information that is confidential and proprietary to Andson Research Ltd.

Table of Contents

8. Significant Findings from Interventional Clinical Trials
9. Observational and Epidemiological Studies
10. Other Information
    10.1 Lack of Efficacy
    10.2 Chemistry, Manufacturing, and Formulation Issues
    10.3 Non-Clinical Findings
    10.4 Literature
11. Information from Marketing Experience
12. Late Breaking Information
13. Overall Safety Evaluation
14. Summary of Important Risks
15. New Actions Recommended
16. Conclusions

Appendices to DSUR

Appendix A: Inventory of Ongoing and Completed Interventional Clinical Trials
Appendix B: DCSI Available at Beginning of Report Period
Appendix C: Line Listings
Appendix D: Cumulative Summary Tabulation
Appendix E: Cumulative Summary Tabulations by Indication
Appendix F: Cumulative Summary Tabulations by Formulation

Executive Summary

This developmental safety update report (DSUR) on qweasytrol hydrochloride dihydrate (i.e., qweasytrol) is in the format proposed by the CIOMS VII Working Group. It summarizes the safety data received by Andson Research Ltd., from worldwide sources, between 14-Jul-2005 and 13-Jul-2006. This is the fourth DSUR for qweasytrol prepared by Andson Research Limited.

Qweasytrol is a highly selective epsilon-G_2 receptor antagonist. It is being studied for the prevention of nausea and vomiting associated with motion sickness, for the symptomatic treatment of nausea and vertigo associated with Ménières disease and other labyrinthine disturbances, and for the treatment of nausea and vomiting associated with gastrointestinal disorders and cytotoxic chemotherapy. The European Institute of Metabolic Diseases is an independent non-commercial sponsor of a Phase II interventional clinical trial investigating qweasytrol for the prophylaxis of acute neurological attacks in patients with porphyria variegate. It is estimated, based on an accounting of unblinded completed studies and the enrolment and allocation schedule for blinded ongoing studies, that the numbers of patients exposed to qweasytrol during the period of this DSUR and cumulatively were approximately 640 and 1992, respectively.

During the reporting period of this DSUR, the following safety related updates (*updates in italics*) were added to the Development Core Safety Information (DCSI) for qweasytrol (see Sections 4, 8 and 10.3 of this DSUR). The Investigator's Brochure (IB), informed consent, Development Risk Management Plan, and study protocols were updated to reflect this information, as appropriate.

- **Contraindications**
  Patients with a history of urticaria related to any prior drug treatments.
  Patients with hepatic disease, including hepatitis and cirrhosis
  Patients with a creatinine clearance $\leq$ *20 mL/min*

- **Precautions**
  A pharmacokinetic interaction study showed that an elevation of serum digoxin levels may occur among patients receiving concomitant qweasytrol and digoxin. In patients receiving treatment with digoxin, serum levels of digoxin should be closely monitored, especially during the first 2 weeks after initiating therapy with qweasytrol.

  Serum creatinine levels should be monitored at every visit. Treatment with qweasytrol should be immediately discontinued in patients who experience a 50% increase in serum creatinine levels. Patients with qweasytrol should be adequately hydrated. Reintroduction of qweasytrol should be considered only when serum creatinine levels have returned to baseline.

- **Suspected Serious Adverse Reactions**
  The following suspected serious adverse reactions have been observed in clinical trials in patients receiving treatment with qweasytrol:
  - *Urticaria*
  - *Hepatitis*
  - *Renal insufficiency*

- **Non-Clinical Studies**
  Results of a non-clinical reproductive toxicity study demonstrated that among mice exposed to qweasytrol (1200 mg/kg) throughout gestation, increased rates of foetal death were observed as were

renal cysts, and renal degeneration among newborn offspring. The significance of these results and their relevance to exposure among humans has yet to be clarified.

The occurrence of acute renal insufficiency was 1.3% of qweasytrol patients vs. 0.6% of placebo patients (P<0.01) enrolled in study A-005 for the prevention of nausea and vomiting associated with gastrointestinal disorders and chemotherapy. Based on these results, and considering the benefit-risk considerations and practical difficulties in monitoring renal function in patients with less severe illnesses (motion sickness, Ménières disease, and other labyrinthine disturbances), as well as the availability of alternative therapies, we have decided to suspend temporarily the ongoing clinical trials in the latter indications until the renal insufficiency is better understood. However, clinical development will continue in gastrointestinal disorders, chemotherapy-induced nausea and vomiting, and porphyria variegate.

Two (2) reports of transient blindness among patients in study A-005 who received high doses of qweasytrol (30 mg tablet) were evaluated as non-causally related by the study investigators. Both subjects had metastatic carcinoma and were receiving cytotoxic chemotherapy. The clinical courses of these patients and the potential seriousness of these events led to the selection of transient blindness as an ADR of Special Interest. Any future reports will be closely scrutinized and followed-up using a special survey form that is currently under development.

Reports of haemolytic anaemia among patients receiving blinded IV injection treatment have been observed in interventional clinical trials. New adverse event reports of haemolytic anaemia will be closely monitored and if necessary, the Development Risk Management Plan for qweasytrol will be updated. A specific adverse event form will be developed in order to investigate this event more precisely.

After the data lock point for this DSUR the Company received a report of a spontaneous abortion in a female patient exposed to tablet qweasytrol. The clinical significance, if any, of this finding in light of the results of a preclinical toxicity study that demonstrated adverse pregnancy outcomes among mice is not known. The risk in pregnancy is being assessed and Andson Research Ltd. will take all the necessary measures to manage the potential risks, including additional reproductive toxicology studies in rats and monkeys.

An evaluation of manufacturing stability data demonstrated that both the tablet and intravenous (IV) injection formulation of qweasytrol should be stored at temperatures below 30ºC. At temperatures above 45ºC, there is a time-dependent degradation of the active moiety of qweasytrol. In addition, an evaluation of formulation data demonstrated that both tablet and IV forms of qweasytrol should be protected from natural and artificial light while stored, since there is a time-dependent degradation of the active moiety with exposure to light.

On 11-Jun-2006 Andson Research Ltd. was granted its first marketing authorization approval for qweasytrol in Mexico. The data lock point for future reports will now transition from the Development International Birth Date (DIBD) of 14-Jul-2002 to the International Birth Date (IBD) of 11-Jun-2006.

1. Introduction

This development safety update report (DSUR) on qweasytrol hydrochloride dihydrate (i.e., qweasytrol) is in the format proposed by the CIOMS VII Working Group. It summarizes the safety data received by Andson Research Ltd., from worldwide sources, between 14-Jul-2005 and 13-Jul-2006. This is the fourth annual DSUR for qweasytrol prepared by Andson Research Ltd. The DIBD for qweasytrol is 14-Jul-2002.

Andson Research Ltd. is the exclusive worldwide commercial sponsor of the development programme for qweasytrol. Qweasytrol is a highly selective epsilon-G_2 receptor antagonist. As of the data lock point for this DSUR, Andson Research Ltd. had completed five (5) studies, including three (3) that were completed during the period of this DSUR. Ongoing studies with qweasytrol include one (1) Phase II interventional clinical trial for the prevention of vomiting associated with motion sickness, and two (2) Phase III interventional clinical trials for the symptomatic treatment of nausea and vertigo associated with Ménières disease, and for the treatment of nausea and vomiting associated with cytotoxic chemotherapy.

The European Institute of Metabolic Diseases is an independent non-commercial sponsor of a Phase II interventional clinical trial investigating qweasytrol for the prophylaxis of acute neurological attacks in patients with porphyria variegate (Study SAB-218). All relevant safety data from this trial are available to Andson Research Ltd., and are presented in this DSUR.

On 11-Jun-2006 Andson Research Ltd. was granted its first marketing authorization approval for qweasytrol tablet and IV injection in Mexico. Marketing authorization was granted for the treatment of nausea and vomiting associated with gastrointestinal disorders and cytotoxic chemotherapy. Andson Research Ltd. has since obtained clinical trial authorization in Mexico for one (1) Phase IV interventional clinical trial of qweasytrol in the treatment of nausea and vomiting associated with cytotoxic chemotherapy. No patients are currently enrolled in this planned trial. The product has not yet been launched; therefore, no data on its use in medical practice are available. The data lock point for future reports will now transition from the DIBD of 14-Jul-2002 to the IBD of 11-Jun-2006. Therefore, the next DSUR (number 5) will cover the period from 14-Jul-2006 to and including 10-Jun-2007.

2. Worldwide Market Authorization Status

At the time of this report qweasytrol (under the Worldwide Trade name of EMNO™) had been granted marketing authorization approval in one (1) country (see Table 2.1), although the product has yet to be launched. With the granting of marketing authorization the Development Risk Management Plan for qweasytrol will form the basis for a Post-Marketing Development Risk Management Plan. There are no records of any registration being restricted, revoked or withdrawn for safety reasons. There are no records of failure to obtain marketing authorization due to a safety concern.

Table 2.1 Qweasytrol Worldwide Market Authorization Status

Country	Approval Date	Launch Date	Trade-name	Formulation(s)	Indication
Mexico	11-Jun-2006	*Pending*	EMNO™	Tablet IV injection	Treatment of nausea and vomiting associated with gastrointestinal disorders and cytotoxic chemotherapy

3. Update on Actions Taken for Safety Reasons

As a result of four new suspected serious adverse reactions that were observed during the period of this report, the DCSI (see section 4), Investigators Brochure (IB), informed consent information, Development Risk Management Plan, and study protocols were updated to reflect this information, as appropriate. The new suspected adverse reactions were: urticaria, hepatitis, drug interaction with digoxin, and renal insufficiency. Details for these suspected reactions are found in section 8.

All protocols have been amended to exclude patients with pre-existing hepatic disease, and to closely monitor digoxin levels in patients requiring concomitant digoxin. In addition, the following requirements have been added as a result of the renal insufficiency cases: patients with a creatinine clearance $\leq$ 20mL/min should be excluded from studies. Patients should be adequately hydrated before receiving qweasytrol. Serum creatinine levels should be monitored at every visit. Treatment with qweasytrol should be discontinued immediately in patients who experience a 50% increase in serum creatinine levels. Reintroduction of qweasytrol should be considered only when serum creatinine levels have returned to baseline.

We have informed all relevant regulatory authorities of the renal insufficiency findings and have provided them with a summary of the final report of study A-005.

Based on the results of a non-clinical reproductive toxicity study (see section 10.3) which showed that mice exposed to qweasytrol (1200 mg/kg) throughout gestation had increased rates of foetal death, and increased incidences of renal cysts and renal degeneration among offspring, the DCSI (see section 4), the IB, informed consent information, and Development Risk Management Plan for qweasytrol were updated to reflect this information. The significance of these results and their relevance to exposure among humans have yet to be clarified. Investigational site personnel have been instructed to advise patients of childbearing potential and to ensure that adequate birth control measures are taken during participation in each clinical trial.

4. Changes to Reference Safety Information

The DCSI for qweasytrol that was available at beginning of the report period is attached as Appendix B.

During the reporting period of this DSUR, the following safety related updates (*updates in italics*) were added to the DCSI (see Sections 8 and 10.3 of this DSUR). The IB, informed consent, Development Risk Management Plan, and study protocols were also updated to reflect this information, where appropriate.

- **Contraindications**
  Patients with a history of urticaria related to any prior drug treatments.

Patients with hepatic disease, including hepatitis and cirrhosis.
Patients with a creatinine clearance $\leq$ *20 mL/min*

- **Precautions**
  A pharmacokinetic interaction study showed that an elevation of serum digoxin levels may occur among patients receiving concomitant treatment with both qweasytrol and digoxin. In patients receiving treatment with digoxin, serum levels of digoxin should be closely monitored, especially during the first 2 weeks after initiating therapy with qweasytrol.

  Serum creatinine levels should be monitored at every visit. Patients should be adequately hydrated before receiving qweasytrol. Treatment with qweasytrol should be immediately discontinued in patients who experience a 50% increase in serum creatinine levels. Reintroduction of qweasytrol should be considered only when serum creatinine levels have returned to baseline.

- **Suspected Serious Adverse Reactions**
  The following serious adverse reactions have been observed in clinical trials among patients receiving treatment with qweasytrol:
  - *Urticaria*
  - *Hepatitis*
  - *Renal insufficiency*

- **Non-clinical Studies**
  Results of a preclinical toxicity study demonstrated that among mice exposed to qweasytrol (1200 mg/kg) throughout gestation, increased rates of foetal death were observed as were renal cysts, and renal degeneration among newborn offspring. The significance of these results and their relevance to exposure among humans have yet to be clarified.

5. Inventory and Status of Ongoing and Completed Interventional Clinical Trials

At the time of this report, qweasytrol has been the focus of ten (10) clinical trials including three (3) Phase I, one (1) Phase II , and one (1) Phase III clinical trials that have been completed plus two (2) Phase II[1] and two (2)

[1] The European Institute of Metabolic Diseases is the non-commercial sponsor of one (1) of the two ongoing Phase II interventional clinical trials (Study SAB-218).

Phase III clinical trials that are currently ongoing. One (1) Phase IV trial is currently authorized although no patients have been randomized to treatment at the time of this DSUR.

The administrative information for these trials is summarized in Appendix A.

6. Estimated Patient Exposure in Clinical Trials

Overall, the number of patients who were enrolled in the qweasytrol clinical programme described in Section 5 and Appendix A of this DSUR was approximately 4568. Of these, it is estimated that 1832 were enrolled during the period of this DSUR. Estimates of patient exposure in Table 6.1, for both the period of this DSUR and cumulatively, are based on unblinded completed studies and the enrollment and randomization schemes for blinded ongoing studies. It is estimated that the numbers of patients exposed to qweasytrol during the period of this DSUR and cumulatively were approximately 640 and 1992, respectively. Based on study designs, most patients in completed studies (other than Phase 1) were treated for 52 weeks. Most patients in ongoing studies are to be treated for 20 weeks.

Table 6.1 Estimated Patient Exposure in Interventional Clinical Trials

	DSUR Period	Cumulative
Treatment	#	#
qweasytrol	640 (598 PO; 42 IV)	1992 (1640 PO; 352 IV)
diphenhydramine	276	344
metoclopramide	276	344
placebo	640 (589 PO; 51 IV)	1888 (1587 PO; 301 IV)
TOTAL	**1832**	**4568**

As noted in Section 10.3 (Non-Clinical Findings) of this DSUR, there is interest in the potential for exposure of females of childbearing potential. An estimate of cumulative enrolment by age for all female patients enrolled in the clinical trials is presented in Table 6.2 for all treatment groups. These data highlight the current limitations of drug exposure experience among younger females of childbearing potential. As this dataset increases with additional clinical experience, future DSURs will present updates to these estimates, as deemed appropriate and necessary.

Table 6.2 Estimated Cumulative Female Enrollment for All Treatments by Age in All Qweasytrol Interventional Clinical Trials	
Age (yr)	**Number**
< 15	0
16 – 20	0
21 – 25	52
26 – 30	56
31 – 35	122
36 – 40	258
41 – 45	594
46 – 50	386
51 – 55	236
56 – 60	97
61 – 65	73
66 – 70	98
71 – 80	0
> 80	0
TOTAL	**1972**

7. Presentation of Safety Data from Clinical Studies

General Considerations

Data on serious[2] individual case reports are presented from clinical trials worldwide of qweasytrol, published and unpublished, received by Andson Research Ltd., both during the reporting period of 14-Jul-2005 to 13-Jul-2006 and cumulatively since the DIBD of 14-Jul-2002. The criteria for case inclusion are described below. The adverse event terminologies displayed are preferred terms from the Medical Dictionary for Regulatory Activities (MedDRA) version 9.0. Andson Research Ltd. is the exclusive worldwide commercial sponsor of the development programme for qweasytrol.[3]

"Expectedness" for qweasytrol cases is based on the DCSI that was available at the start of the report period. "Expectedness" for marketed comparator cases is based on the versions of the European Union Summary of Product Characteristics (EU-SPC) that were available for each product at the start of the report period. For blinded reports, "expectedness" is based on the DCSI for qweasytrol that was available at the start of the report period.

[2] As defined under ICH Guideline E2A

[3] Individual case reports from the study sponsored by the European Institute of Metabolic Diseases are included.

Line Listings

The line listings present individual case reports with at least one suspected unexpected serious adverse reaction (SUSAR) that were first received during this reporting period. Causal-relationship was judged as related to treatment by either the investigator or the sponsor (or both). The SUSARs in Appendix C of this DSUR are designated with an asterisk (*) in order to distinguish them from "non-SUSAR events" associated with the same individual case reports. The ADRs of Special Interest[4] in Appendix C of this DSUR are designated with a cross (†). The line listings present data from the entire clinical trial development programme for qweasytrol and then are sorted by treatment. The individual case reports are assigned to the MedDRA system organ class (SOC) of the most clinically significant ADR term, which is underlined.

Summary Tabulations

Cumulative summary tabulations are presented for the period from the DIBD for qweasytrol to the data lock point of this DSUR (14-Jul-2002 to 13-Jul-2006) in Appendices D, E, and F. The summary tabulations present all serious adverse events from individual case reports that were judged serious, as well as AEs of Special Interest. They are sorted primarily by treatment (i.e., qweasytrol, comparator, placebo, blinded). The ADRs that were originally SUSARs are designated with an asterisk (*) in Appendices D, E, and F. The ADRs of Special Interest[4] are designated with a cross (†). Due to the interim nature of these data, this tabulation may include data from ongoing clinical trials whose data may not have been completely validated.

- Appendix D presents cumulative data across the entire development programme for qweasytrol.
- Appendix E presents cumulative data by indication: porphyria variegate versus all other indications (motion sickness, Ménières Disease, gastrointestinal disorders, and nausea due to cytotoxic chemotherapy). These are presented separately because: 1) patients with porphyria variegate receive qweasytrol 400 mg daily, whereas the dose is 30 mg daily for all other indications; 2) porphyria variegate differs from the other indications in terms of the type and incidence

[4] Includes the following MedDRA preferred terms: blind spot enlarged, blindness, blindness cortical, blindness day, blindness night, blindness NOS, blindness transient, blindness unilateral, vision blurred, visual acuity reduced, visual acuity reduced transiently, visual acuity tests abnormal, visual field defect, visual field defect NOS, visual field tests abnormal.

of background adverse events; and 3) the porphyria variegate study is being conducted by an independent organization.

- Appendix F presents cumulative data by formulation (tablet and IV injection). These are separated because of significant differences between the two routes in terms of pharmacokinetics and pharmacodynamics.

Published Literature

During the period of the DSUR two (2) individual case reports were described in the published literature. Both cases were already submitted to regulators as unblinded cases (SUSARs) and are included in the attached cumulative summary tabulations. These individual case reports describe patients from the completed and unblinded study #A-005 who developed transient blindness after exposure to 30 mg tablet of qweasytrol. A study investigator was the primary author of these publications (see Section 10.4). The experiences of these two (2) subjects led to the selection of several ADRs of Special Interest, as listed in footnote 4.

Company Reference Number for Patient	Literature Reference
AR-103856	Clifton, A. *et al., J. Nausea* 374 (4): 212, 2006
AR-104734	Clifton, A. *et al., Int. J. Emesis* 32 (1): 1717, 2006

8. Significant Findings from Interventional Clinical Trials

8.1 Completed Studies

Clinical study synopses from three (3) studies of qweasytrol that were completed during the period of this DSUR are presented below and include a discussion of the significant findings.

Study A-003

Study Title: Pharmacokinetic interaction study with digoxin

Clinical Study Type: Phase I

Study Status: complete

Study Rationale: Investigate potential for drug interaction between qweasytrol and digoxin

Number & Location Study Centres: three (3): UK, USA, Mexico

Study Design: randomized, open-label, crossover, placebo-controlled

Dosage Form: tablet, IV injection

Investigational Drug: 10 mg tablet, 2 mg IV qweasytrol

Reference Therapy: placebo

Number of Subjects: 67

Demographics of Population: 35 male, 32 female

Main Criteria for Inclusion: healthy, adult

Main Criteria for Exclusion: no concomitant therapy within 14 days

Duration of Subject Participation: 90 days

Duration of Study: 125 days

Method of Evaluation: observation, patient reporting of AEs, analysis of blood and urine

Pharmacokinetics Results: Qweasytrol tablet increased the pharmacokinetic parameters $AUC_{0\text{-}24hr}$ and C_{max} for digoxin by 7% and 14%, respectively, at Day 10 of treatment, and by 12% and 16%, respectively, at Day 30 of treatment. Qweasytrol IV injection increased the pharmacokinetic parameters $AUC_{0\text{-}24hr}$ and C_{max} for digoxin by 13% and 17%, respectively, at Day 10 of treatment, and by 18% and 20%, respectively, at Day 30 of treatment. Patients appeared to be at the greatest risk for developing elevated serum digoxin levels during the first two weeks after initiating treatment with qweasytrol.

Efficacy Results: Not applicable

Safety Results: No serious adverse experiences or ADRs were observed during the study.

Conclusion: The results of this study demonstrate that the potential exists for a clinically significant interaction between qweasytrol and digoxin. Digoxin levels should be monitored carefully in patients receiving concomitant qweasytrol.

Study A-004

Study Title: Safety & Efficacy of Qweasytrol in Labyrinthine Disturbances

Clinical Study Type: Phase II

Study Status: complete

Study Rationale: To investigate the safety and efficacy of a highly selective epsilon-G_2 receptor antagonist in the symptomatic treatment of nausea and vertigo associated with labyrinthine disturbances.

Number & Location Study Centres: seven (7): UK (3), USA (3), Mexico (1)

Study Design: Randomized, double-blind, placebo controlled

Dosage Form: tablet

Investigational Drug: 10 mg qweasytrol

Reference Therapy: n/a

Number of Subjects: 110 (1:1 randomization scheme: 57 qweasytrol, 53 placebo)

Demographics of Population: 47 male, 63 female

Main Criteria for Inclusion: adult, nausea and/or vertigo of more than 5 days duration

Main Criteria for Exclusion: prior or current diagnosis of carcinoma, concurrent anti-emetic therapy

Duration of Subject Participation: 12 weeks

Duration of Study: 26 weeks

Method of Evaluation: patient self reports, visual analogue scale assessments of nausea and vertigo

Pharmacokinetics Results: Not applicable

Efficacy Results: In an intent-to-treat analysis patients receiving qweasytrol experience significant ($P<.05$) reductions in nausea and vertigo after 5 days of treatment compared to patients receiving placebo.

Safety Results: Clinical adverse experiences were reported by 24 of the subjects. Two (2) patients experienced serious ADRs, including one (1) report each of hematuria and blurred vision among patients treated with placebo.

Conclusion: In a placebo-controlled study qweasytrol was both efficacious and well tolerated in the short-term treatment of nausea and vertigo associated with labyrinthine disturbances.

Study A-005

Study Title: Qweasytrol in the Treatment of Nausea and Vomiting Associated with Gastrointestinal Disorders and Chemotherapy

Clinical Study Type: Phase III

Study Status: complete

Study Rationale: To investigate the safety and efficacy of a highly selective epsilon-G_2 receptor antagonist in the symptomatic treatment of nausea and vomiting associated with gastrointestinal disorders and chemotherapy.

Number & Location Study Centres: 17: Mexico (2), South Africa (2), Canada (4), France (9)

Study Design: Randomized, double blind, placebo controlled study. Two discreet patient populations were studied: 1) Chemotherapy patients received a regimen that included cisplatin ≥70 mg/m^2 in combination with an ondansetron/dexamethasone regimen, and were randomized (1:1) to qweasytrol 10 mg or placebo (IV injection). The dose could be increased to 30 mg (or matching placebo) if symptoms were not adequately controlled. 2) Patients with non-parasitic gastrointestinal disease were randomized (1:1) to qweasytrol or placebo (PO).

Dosage Form: tablet, IV injection

Investigational Drug: qweasytrol: 10, 30 mg tablets; 2 mg IV

Reference Therapy: Not applicable

Number of Subjects: 2786 (1:1 randomization scheme: 1088 qweasytrol tablet, 1080 placebo tablet, 317 qweasytrol IV, 301 placebo IV)

Demographics of Population: 1683 male, 1103 female

Main Criteria for Inclusion: adults with nausea and/or vomiting of more than 10 days duration associated with chemotherapy or non-parasitic gastrointestinal disease.

Main Criteria for Exclusion: advanced renal or hepatic disease, dementia

Duration of Subject Participation: 52 weeks

Duration of Study: 2 years

Method of Evaluation: patient self reports, visual analogue scale assessments of nausea, patient diaries of emetic episodes

Pharmacokinetics Results: Not applicable

Efficacy Results: For both patient populations, a total of 2786 patients (1394 assigned qweasytrol, 1392 placebo) were included in the intent-to-treat analysis. Treatment with qweasytrol was associated with a significant ($P<0.01$) reduction in nausea and vomiting, compared to treatment with placebo. These benefits persisted ($P<0.01$) among patients who continued treatment for up to 1 year.

Safety Results: Clinical adverse experiences were reported by 13% of the subjects. Among subjects treated with oral qweasytrol (or oral placebo), renal insufficiency was observed in 26 patients (18 in the qweasytrol group vs. 8 in the placebo group, 1.3% vs. 0.6%, respectively, $P<0.01$). Two (2) qweasytrol patients experienced urticaria that was rated by the investigator as drug-related. One (1) placebo patient experienced urticaria. One (1) qweasytrol patient experienced hepatitis that was rated by the investigator as drug-related. The patient (AR-102856) was receiving concomitant treatment with hydrochlorothiazide. When qweasytrol was discontinued (hydrochlorothiazide was continued), the patient recovered. There were no cases of hepatitis among placebo patients. Two (2) patients who received high doses of qweasytrol experienced transient blindness that was assessed by the investigators as not related to treatment. Both subjects had metastatic carcinoma and were receiving cytotoxic chemotherapy.

Conclusion: Qweasytrol is effective in the treatment of nausea and vomiting associated with gastrointestinal disorders and chemotherapy. Potential safety issues requiring monitoring include urticaria, hepatitis, transient blindness, and renal insufficiency.

8.2 Ongoing Studies

There were some preliminary findings involving clinically important safety signals from studies ongoing during this DSUR period.

Exposure During Pregnancy

One (1) unblinded report was received of a spontaneous abortion in a subject who received qweasytrol while enrolled in clinical trial A-006 (see Sections 12 and 13).

Urticaria

One (1) unblinded case report from clinical trial A-007 documented serious urticaria in a patient receiving qweasytrol, who had a history of drug-related urticaria (see Section 13).

Visual Events

One (1) unblinded case of blurred vision (i.e., an ADR of Special Interest) was reported in a patient receiving qweasytrol in the study SAB-219 (see Section 13).

Haemolytic Anaemia

Haemolytic anaemia was observed in two (2) patients who received blinded treatment via IV injection in study A-008 (see Section 13).

9. Observational and Epidemiological Studies

At the time of this DSUR no observational or epidemiological studies with qweasytrol have been conducted, analyzed, or completed.

The European Institute of Metabolic Diseases, which is the non-commercial sponsor of a Phase II interventional clinical trial investigating qweasytrol for the prophylaxis of acute neurological attacks in patients with porphyria variegate, is currently planning an epidemiology study of that indication. This study will be designed to characterize the natural history of the disease using data collected from five (5) African countries: Cameroon, Kenya, South Africa, Tanzania, and Zambia. This will be a non-interventional study and as such, no patients will be randomized to any treatment, including qweasytrol. When available, data from this epidemiology study will be presented in the DSUR from Andson Research Ltd.

10. Other Information

10.1 Lack of Efficacy

No data were obtained suggesting a lack of efficacy that would constitute a significant risk to the study population.

10.2 Chemistry, Manufacturing, and Formulation Issues

An evaluation of manufacturing stability data demonstrated that both the tablet and intravenous (IV) injection formulation of qweasytrol should be stored at temperatures below 30°C. At temperatures above 45°C there is a time-dependent degradation of the active moiety. In addition, an evaluation of formulation data demonstrated that both tablet and IV forms of qweasytrol should be protected from natural and artificial light while stored, since there is a time-dependent degradation of the active moiety with exposure to light.

10.3 Non-Clinical Findings

A non-clinical reproductive toxicity study in mice exposed to qweasytrol (1200 mg/kg) throughout gestation revealed increased rates of foetal death (37% qweasytrol vs. 6% placebo). Among surviving newborns, renal cysts (23% qweasytrol vs. 2% placebo), and renal degeneration (18% qweasytrol vs. 1% placebo) were observed by 6-months of age.

10.4 Literature

One (1) published abstract (Starlet, T. *Arch. Emesis* 83 (2):27, 2006) described a study with potentially important safety information regarding qweasytrol. This *in vitro* study examined the influence of four (4) different epsilon-G_2 receptor antagonists, including qweasytrol, on renal glomerular ionic permeability in isolated rat glomeruli. Exposure to any of the tested epsilon-G_2 receptor antagonists resulted in dose-dependant reductions in glomerular permeability to Ca^{++} and Na^{++}. Changes in glomerular ionic permeability could have detrimental effects on renal structure and function. A copy of the published abstract is appended to this DSUR.[5]

During the period of the DSUR two (2) unblinded individual case reports (AR-103856, AR-104734) of transient blindness from study A-005 were subsequently described in the published literature (see Section 7).

11. Information from Marketing Experience

There is no marketing experience to date.

12. Late Breaking Information

After the data lock point of this DSUR, follow-up to an initial report (A-105957) presented in this DSUR (#4) was received. This 35-year-old female patient is enrolled in clinical trial A-006 (Safety & Efficacy of Qweasytrol in the Prevention of Vomiting Associated with Motion Sickness). The patient was reported to have conceived while receiving blinded study therapy. It is estimated that the patient received blinded study therapy from 1 week prior to conception through week 3 of gestation. At 5 weeks of gestation the patient experienced a spontaneous abortion. The study blind was broken and it was determined that the patient had been treated with qweasytrol.

13. Overall Safety Evaluation

13.1 Prior Experience

Previously recognized ADRs with qweasytrol treatment include drowsiness, headache, diarrhoea, and rash. These ADRs are listed in the DCSI. During the period of this DSUR no relevant new or follow-up information regarding these risks was identified.

---

[5] *Note for the reader*: A copy of the abstract is not appended to this sample DSUR, but would be for a real DSUR.

13.2 Evaluation of the Risks

Overall Safety Experience

In completed, unblinded clinical trials, the overall incidence of side effects reported with qweasytrol was comparable with that of placebo, with one important exception (renal insufficiency; see below). Side effects with qweasytrol were generally mild and rarely required discontinuation of therapy. Several safety issues were identified, including serious adverse experiences that were rated as drug-related by the investigators. In addition, non-drug related reports of "transient blindness" that were identified during the period of this DSUR were the subject of increased scrutiny.

The cumulative incidences of serious adverse events, including both those that are expected (listed) and unexpected (unlisted), were similar for patients treated with qweasytrol and placebo (see Appendix D). Analyses of these reports and comparisons of these data to the cumulative incidences for blinded reports and reports for active comparators (e.g., metoclopramide, diphenhydramine) did not reveal any new general safety concerns.

Death

To date, none of the fatalities that have been observed among patients enrolled in clinical trials of qweasytrol was characterized as being causally related to treatment by either the investigators or the sponsor. All reported fatalities (n = 6) have occurred among patients with carcinoma who were receiving cytotoxic chemotherapy. This includes patients from completed clinical trials who received qweasytrol (2) or placebo (3), as well as one (1) non-drug related fatality (treatment currently blinded) from an ongoing study.

Renal insufficiency

During this period the most significant safety issue has been the occurrence of acute renal insufficiency in study A-005. In this completed Phase III study, the incidence of acute renal insufficiency was significantly higher for qweasytrol versus placebo (1.3% vs. 0.6%, $P<0.01$). To date, all patients who received qweasytrol in clinical trials and developed renal insufficiency (n = 18) have recovered without sequelae after discontinuation of treatment. Typical time to complete recovery was 4-5 weeks. A review of all completed and unblinded studies identified no other serious reports of renal insufficiency among patients treated with either qweasytrol or placebo. The incidences of all renal function laboratory abnormalities across the entire development programme were similar between patients treated with qweasytrol (2.1%) and placebo (1.8%). Several steps have been taken (section 3) and will be taken (section 15) to understand and manage this risk.

Hepatitis

Three (3) subjects have had SUSARs for hepatitis and/or elevated transaminases. There was one (1) qweasytrol-related hepatitis case in completed study A-005, and two SUSARs for elevated hepatic transaminases to date in the ongoing study A-006 (these subjects were found to be taking qweasytrol when unblinded). All 3 cases were judged to be causally related to qweasytrol. In each case the patients were receiving 10 mg qweasytrol tablets for approximately 3 to 4 weeks prior to the onset of hepatic changes. The patient who developed hepatitis (AR-102856) was receiving concomitant treatment with hydrochlorothiazide. Treatment with qweasytrol was discontinued (hydrochlorothiazide was continued) and the patient recovered. One of the two patients in study A-006 (AR-101454) developed elevations in alanine aminotransferase but recovered with continued treatment. A patient who developed elevations in aspartate aminotransferase was suspected of excessive alcohol intake (AR-101667). Treatment with qweasytrol was discontinued and the patient recovered. A review of data from completed and unblinded studies identified no other reports of hepatitis. Four (4) non-serious, non-drug related reports of elevated hepatic enzymes were identified including, three (3) among subjects treated with qweasytrol and one (1) with placebo.

Overdose

Previously recognized risks with qweasytrol treatment include the potential for patient misuse and overdose with the tablet formulation as patients could conceivably overmedicate due to a perceived delay while awaiting the onset of action. At the time of this DSUR four (4) subjects who were enrolled in completed clinical studies were found to have overdosed with qweasytrol. In 3 of these cases the overdoses were single, acute exposures, with 2 patients reporting no adverse effects and one (1) patient reporting headache and nausea. In one (1) case the overdosing was chronic, being of more than one day in duration. The subject who inadvertently received double the intended dose of qweasytrol per day (20 mg PO) reported headache and diarrhoea. The cumulative experience as of the data lock point of this DSUR has not led to the identification of any new or previously unrecognized risks associated with qweasytrol overdose.

Drug Interaction

A pharmacokinetic interaction study (A-003) showed that an elevation of serum digoxin levels may occur among patients receiving concomitant treatment with both qweasytrol and digoxin. The mechanism by which qweasytrol influences circulating levels of digoxin is not currently understood. Qweasytrol is not an inducer or inhibitor of cytochrome P450, and would therefore not be expected to affect other drugs which are substrates of cytochrome P450. *In vitro* drug interaction studies with qweasytrol and lithium, HMG-CoA reductase inhibitors, thiazide diuretics, oral contraceptives, warfarin, anticonvulsants, and calcium channel blockers have not identified any other interactions. As of the data lock point of this DSUR, no drug-related reports of drug interaction have been identified with qweasytrol, active comparators, or placebo.

Exposure During Pregnancy

Prior to the period covered by this DSUR, there was no experience with exposure to qweasytrol during pregnancy. Single-dose and multiple-dose pre-clinical toxicity studies in mice and rats yielded similar results with qweasytrol and placebo. Results of a long-term, high-dose, reproductive toxicity study during the period of this DSUR demonstrated adverse pregnancy outcomes in mice. The relevance of these findings and of the single case of a spontaneous abortion in a 35 year-old female treated with qweasytrol (see section 12) is unknown.

Visual Events

Two (2) reports of transient blindness among patients in study A-005 who received high doses of qweasytrol (30 mg tablet) were evaluated as non-causally related by the study investigators (AR-103856, AR-104734). Both subjects had metastatic carcinoma and were receiving cytotoxic chemotherapy. The clinical courses of these patients, including time-to-onset after initiating high-dose (30 mg) oral therapy (i.e., within 2 weeks of initiating treatment), and the potential gravity of this event led to the selection of related ADRs of Special Interest[4] for qweasytrol. These two (2) cases were subsequently described in the published literature (see section 7). To date, no reports of transient blindness have been identified among any patients receiving active comparators or placebo.

During the period of this DSUR one (1) case of blurred vision (i.e., an ADR of Special Interest) was observed in a patient receiving 400 mg of qweasytrol daily for the treatment of porphyria variegate (unblinded report S2754 from study SAB-219). No other reports of visual disturbances have been observed among subjects receiving qweasytrol, active comparators, or placebo in these clinical studies. There have been no pre-clinical findings suggestive of ocular effects of qweasytrol. The significance, if any, of this finding in light of two (2) earlier cases of transient blindness, is currently not known.

Urticaria

During this period two (2) unblinded urticaria reports (AR-101688, AR-101598) from completed study A-005 were judged causally-related to qweasytrol (10 mg tablet daily) and one (1) patient who was treated with placebo in study A-005 experienced urticaria that was rated as causally related by the investigator. AR-101598 had recently experienced a respiratory infection while AR-101688 had a history of unspecified drug allergy. In addition, during the period of this DSUR an unblinded case report from the ongoing clinical trial A-007 demonstrated that a patient (AR-101632) with a history of urticaria while receiving prior treatment with an angiotension converting enzyme inhibitor subsequently experienced serious urticaria while receiving treatment with qweasytrol (10 mg tablet daily). All three patients recovered after qweasytrol was discontinued and with the administration of antihistamines. These data suggest that treatment with qweasytrol may be associated with the development of urticaria and that prior drug-related urticaria might be a risk factor for the development of urticaria while receiving qweasytrol. A review of the cumulative unblinded serious and non-serious adverse event reports to date did not identify signs or symptoms suggestive of urticaria.

Haemolytic Anaemia

During the period of this DSUR two (2) cases of haemolytic anaemia were observed among patients on qweasytrol IV injection (study A-008). Both reports are currently blinded and will remain so until the study is completed. Haemolytic anaemia has not been reported in patients receiving the tablet formulation of qweasytrol (or corresponding comparator groups).

Pharmaceutical Issues

There have been no problems observed with the stability and use of trial supplies to date in spite of the new findings regarding temperature and light sensitivity.

13.3 Benefit-Risk Considerations

The new findings relating to renal insufficiency necessitate an indication-by-indication discussion of the acceptability of risk for current and future patients participating in clinical trials. The other suspected adverse reactions discussed above do not appear to warrant any major changes in the overall benefit-risk perspective for any of the indications.

Prevention and treatment of chemotherapy-induced nausea and vomiting

Severe and/or prolonged episodes of nausea and vomiting may be associated with significant morbidity and may contribute towards increased mortality in severely ill patients. The results from studies A-005 (completed; see section 8.1) and A-008 (ongoing) are consistent with the efficacy of qweasytrol as anticipated at the start of the clinical development programme. The efficacy of the qweasytrol regimen was apparently maintained during all treatment cycles. Considering the potential seriousness of chemotherapy-induced nausea and vomiting, the fact that preliminary results suggest that the acute renal insufficiency induced by qweasytrol may be preventable and reversible, and the reality that chemotherapy patients tend to be intensely monitored, we consider that the benefit-risk balance remains acceptable for continued study of that indication.

Prevention of nausea and vomiting associated with motion sickness; symptomatic treatment of nausea and vertigo associated with Ménières disease and other labyrinthine disturbances

The results from one completed Phase II study (A-004) suggest that qweasytrol demonstrates efficacy for these indications relative to placebo. Using historical controls, efficacy appears to be comparable to existing therapies (analysis available on request). There is one ongoing Phase III study (A-007) in these indications. Based on the occurrence of acute renal insufficiency in 1.3% of qweasytrol patients enrolled in study A-005, the practical difficulties of regular monitoring of renal function in patients treated for these indications, and the availability of alternative therapies, we have decided to suspend temporarily the ongoing clinical trials in these indications. The benefit-risk relationship for qweasytrol patients in these indications will be fully reassessed when the renal toxicity is better understood and characterized.

Prophylaxis of acute neurological attacks in patients with porphyria variegate

Porphyria variegate is prevalent in South Africa. Current treatments include protection of the skin from sunlight and possible use of cholestyramine to decrease photosensitivity. No other treatments are known to have been evaluated for the prophylaxis of acute neurological attacks. Qweasytrol is under study in this indication in a Phase II clinical trial by the European Institute of Metabolic Diseases, who have been informed of the renal insufficiency findings in the Andson Research programme. It is too premature to assess and draw any conclusions concerning the benefit-risk relationship of qweasytrol for this indication. In agreement with the authorities where the trials have been authorized, the European Institute of Metabolic Diseases has decided to complete its ongoing trials in order to re-evaluate the potential benefits of qweasytrol in this indication. The renal function of the patients enrolled in this Phase II trial will be closely monitored. An amendment to their protocol has been submitted to the pertinent regulatory authorities. Andson will maintain close contact with the Institute regarding the ongoing results and will collaborate in assessing the benefit-risk relationship for the indication, especially after further work on the ADR is completed (see section 15).

14. Summary of Important Risks

The known and potential important risks at the time of this DSUR, both previously identified and new, are listed below.

Previously Identified Potential Risks

1. Overdose and Misuse

In the initial emesis prevention studies in dogs and monkeys, a moderate time-to-onset of pharmacologic activity was observed. This moderate time-to-onset for therapeutic effect was observed in studies A-002 and A-004. The potential for patient misuse and overdose with the tablet formulation of qweasytrol was recognized and addressed in the Development Risk Management Plan. Briefly, since the time-to-onset of therapeutic effect for orally-administered qweasytrol may be as long as 60 to 120 minutes, the potential exists for patients to overmedicate while seeking relief from nausea, vomiting, and vertigo. To date, concerns regarding overdose have not been borne out. At the time of this DSUR, the observed cases of overdose have not raised any special safety concerns or signals. Actions previously outlined in the Development Risk Management Plan and taken to reduce the risk of misuse and overdose include the provision of study drug in single-dose blister packs. Currently, it is not felt that there is any specific important and missing safety information on this issue. As outlined in the Development Risk Management Plan, patient-directed interventions will be implemented at the time of market introduction in order to mitigate the potential for inadvertent overdose with qweasytrol. Reports of overdose will be carefully followed up and evaluated.

2. Transient Blindness and Visual ADRs of Special Interest

There is no prior pre-clinical or clinical experience with qweasytrol or other epsilon-G_2 receptor antagonists suggesting a relationship between treatment and the loss of vision. A review of the published scientific literature did not yield any known or hypothetical basis for a relationship between epsilon-G_2 receptor antagonism and visual effects. No adverse effects on the eye were observed in pre-clinical toxicology studies, including high-dose acute studies in mice (AR-01m) and rats (AR-022a) and long-term studies in rats (AR-034a) and dogs (AR-229). While it is possible that metastatic carcinoma, concurrent cytotoxic therapy, or study site/investigator interventions could cause the development of transient blindness (note: both patients were enrolled at the same study site), no specific risk factors have been identified. Due to the serious ramifications of blindness, the observation of two (2) ADRs of transient blindness resulted in the selection of vision-related ADRs as "ADRs of Special Interest."

Newly Identified Risks

3. Renal insufficiency

In one large completed study (A-005), the incidence of acute renal insufficiency was significantly higher for qweasytrol versus placebo (1.3% vs. 0.6%, $P<0.01$). To date, all patients who received qweasytrol in clinical trials and developed renal insufficiency have recovered without sequelae after discontinuation of treatment. Typical time to complete recovery was 4-5 weeks. A review of all completed and unblinded studies identified no other reports of renal insufficiency among patients treated with either qweasytrol or placebo. The incidences of all renal function laboratory abnormalities across the entire development programme were similar between patients treated with qweasytrol (2.1%) and placebo (1.8%). Possible mechanisms are under investigation, including the role of nephrotoxic chemotherapy as a possible contributing factor, the existence of pre-existing renal insufficiency, and the possible contribution of dehydration induced by severe nausea. Several steps have been taken (section 3) and will be taken (section 15) to better understand and manage this risk.

4. Hepatitis

There have been three serious cases of qweasytrol-related hepatitis in the development programme. In each case the patients were receiving 10 mg qweasytrol tablets for approximately 3 to 4 weeks prior to the onset of hepatic changes. Transaminase elevations were not associated with clinical adverse events, and resolved when qweasytrol was discontinued. Epsilon-

G_2 receptor antagonists have not previously been shown to be associated with hepatic toxicity. An *in vitro* toxicology study showed no damage when cultured hepatocytes were incubated with increasing concentrations of qweasytrol. Similarly, in acute and chronic toxicology studies exposure to qweasytrol was not associated with hepatic toxicity at doses as high as 1200 g/kg in mice, rats, and dogs. The DCSI, IB, informed consent, and Development Risk Management Plan for qweasytrol were updated to reflect the observation of serious, drug-related reports of hepatitis and abnormal liver enzymes.

5. Urticaria

An *in vitro* toxicology study showed that qweasytrol can mediate the release of histamine from white blood cells. Due to the possibility of qweasytrol stimulating IgE antibody-mediated hypersensitivity, necropsy tissue samples from an acute dosing study in mice (AM-01b) and a long-term chronic study in rats (AR-02d) were examined for epithelial changes suggestive of hypersensitivity reactions. In these pre-clinical toxicology studies, exposure to qweasytrol was not associated with epithelial or other changes suggestive of hypersensitivity reactions. While rash has previously been observed in clinical trials with qweasytrol, urticaria is a new finding. Similarly, the observation of urticaria in a patient with a history of an unspecified drug allergy highlights the need to identify, if possible, potential risk factors for urticaria. Characterization of urticaria and potential risk factors is currently ongoing via routine monitoring and signal detection techniques.

6. Drug Interaction with Digoxin

During the period of this DSUR, a new risk regarding an interaction between qweasytrol and digoxin was identified following the completion of a pharmacokinetic interaction study (A-003). Initial laboratory studies showed that qweasytrol is not an inducer or inhibitor of cytochrome P450. *In vitro* drug interaction studies with qweasytrol were not suggestive of any clinically important drug interactions. Prior clinical experience with the co-administration of qweasytrol and concomitant therapies has been limited. Subjects taking digoxin will have digoxin levels monitored during participation in clinical trials, and digoxin doses will be adjusted as needed. Although this has the potential to unblind subjects and investigators, it will be an issue in relatively few subjects, and is a necessary measure given the potential risk.

7. Reproductive Toxicity

After the data lock point for this DSUR, Andson received a report of a spontaneous abortion in a female patient exposed to 10 mg tablet qweasytrol (additional details pending). A non-clinical reproductive toxicity study (see section 10.3) showed that mice exposed to qweasytrol (1200 mg/kg) throughout gestation had increased rates of foetal death. The clinical significance of these findings is not known. Epsilon-G_2 receptor antagonists have not previously been shown to be associated with adverse pregnancy outcomes. Single-dose and multiple-dose pre-clinical toxicity studies in mice and rats yielded similar results with qweasytrol and placebo. The risk in pregnancy is being assessed and Andson Research Ltd. will take all the necessary measures to manage the potential risks, including additional reproductive toxicology studies in rats and monkeys.

8. Haemolytic Anaemia

Haemolytic anaemia has been reported in two (2) subjects in clinical trials of IV qweasytrol. Although the cases remain blinded, it is prudent to recognize haemolytic anaemia as a potential risk for patients receiving qweasytrol. There is no prior pre-clinical or clinical experience with qweasytrol and haemolytic anaemia. High-dose acute studies in mice (AR-01m) and rats (AR-022a) and long-term studies in rats (AR-034a) and dogs (AR-229) have not yielded haematology or urinalysis findings that would be suggestive of any haemolytic process. Prior to the observation of these two (2) cases, routine laboratory monitoring has not been suggestive of haemolytic disease in patients enrolled in clinical trials with qweasytrol. Routine laboratory monitoring, with more extensive laboratory investigation for cases of anaemia, should identify any future episodes of haemolytic anaemia. However, no further action regarding these two (2) cases is planned until the blind is broken once the study is completed.

15. New Actions Recommended

The following specific actions have been recommended by Andson Research Ltd. or regulatory authorities to evaluate further and minimize potential and established risks associated with treatment with qweasytrol. Implementation of these actions is in progress. No independent actions have been taken by any regulatory authority, IRB, or DSMB as a result of these or any other issues.

Renal insufficiency

An epidemiological study will be performed in Mexico, where the product is authorized, to estimate the incidence of renal insufficiency and identify potential risk factors. We will investigate the possibility of dose-adjustment in case of worsening of renal function to assess whether or not the occurrence of acute renal insufficiency can be prevented. In addition, as noted in Section 3., for all interventional studies, potential subjects with creatinine clearance < 20mL/min will be excluded from participation. Serum creatinine will be monitored at each visit, and treatment will be suspended in subjects who experience a 50% increase in serum creatinine.

Transient Blindness and Visual ADRs of Special Interest

Andson Research Ltd. will institute special follow-up for any future report of blindness or a visual ADR of special interest. An ADR-specific questionnaire will be developed to investigate this event more precisely.

Haemolytic Anaemia

Hematologic laboratory parameters will be closely monitored, and anaemia adverse events will be investigated closely to determine whether the anaemia is haemolytic in nature. If necessary, the Development Risk Management Plan for qweasytrol will be updated, and a specific adverse event form will be developed in order to investigate this event more fully.

Exposure During Pregnancy

Additional non-clinical toxicity studies in rats and monkeys are being planned in order to obtain safety information that might further an understanding of the potential risks associated with exposure to qweasytrol during pregnancy.

16. Conclusions

In completed, unblinded clinical trials, the overall incidence of side effects reported with qweasytrol was comparable with that of placebo, with the important exception of renal insufficiency.

Additional information obtained since the last DSUR required updating of all relevant documents to be consistent with the current safety profile of qweasytrol. The Development Risk Management Plan has been updated to account for the following: identification of urticaria, hepatitis, and renal insufficiency as possible serious adverse reactions; the need to monitor serum creatinine levels; the need to monitor for elevated serum digoxin levels; exclusion of patients with creatinine clearance ≤ 20 mL/min, prior drug-related urticaria, and pre-existing hepatic disease; and non-clinical reproductive toxicology study findings of adverse pregnancy outcomes in mice exposed to qweasytrol.

As clinical and non-clinical data continue to be collected on the new suspected serious adverse reactions, it will be possible to develop a better understanding of the incidence of these events, as well as risk factors that might be managed. The criteria for an acceptable benefit-risk balance for study participation differ for the distinct populations in the different indications. We conclude that the benefit-risk relationship for qweasytrol trial patients remains positive for the prevention and treatment of chemotherapy induced nausea and vomiting, as well as for the prevention of acute neurological attacks in patients with porphyria variegate.

However, due to the renal insufficiency findings, we have concluded that the clinical trials for the prevention of nausea and vomiting associated with motion sickness, and for the symptomatic treatment of nausea and vertigo associated with Ménières disease and other labyrinthine disturbances, should be suspended until the renal toxicity of qweasytrol is fully understood.

Appendix A

Inventory of Ongoing and Completed Interventional Clinical Trials

Study ID Phase Status	Countries	Trial Title	Design/ Treatment Duration	Dose & Regimen Control Therapy	Trial Population	First Visit First Patient & Planned Enrolment	Interval/ Cumulative Enrolment	Interval/ Cumulative Patient Exposure per Treatment Arm
A-001 Phase I Complete	UK	Safety & Tolerability of AR-708	Open cross-over (double)/ 5 day	5, 10, 30, or 100 mg tablet, 0.5, 1 or 2 mg IV	Healthy, adult volunteers	16-Nov-2002 24	0/24	5 mg tablet: 0/3 10 mg tablet: 0/3 30 mg tablet: 0/4 100 mg tablet: 0/4 0.5 mg IV: 0/3 1 mg IV: 0/3 2 mg IV: 0/4
A-002 Phase I Complete	UK, USA	Pharmacodynamics & Pharmacokinetics of AR-708	Open parallel/ 5 day	30, 100, or 300 mg tablet, 1 or 2 mg IV	Healthy, adult volunteers	25-May-2003 52	0/52	30 mg tablet: 0/12 100 mg tablet: 0/12 300 mg tablet: 0/12 1 mg IV: 0/12 2 mg IV: 0/4
A-003 Phase I Complete	UK, USA, Mexico	A Pharmacokinetic Interaction Study of Qweasytrol and Digoxin.	Randomized, Open cross-over, placebo controlled/ 90 day	10 mg tablet, 2 mg IV	Healthy, adult volunteers	6-Jan-2006 67	67/67	10 mg tablet: 35/35 2 mg IV: 32/32

Study ID Phase Status	Countries	Trial Title	Design/ Treatment Duration	Dose & Regimen Control Therapy	Trial Population	First Visit First Patient & Planned Enrolment	Interval/ Cumulative Enrolment	Interval/ Cumulative Patient Exposure per Treatment Arm
A-004 Phase II Complete	UK, USA, Mexico	Safety & Efficacy of Qweasytrol in Labyrinthine Disturbances	Random-ized, blinded, placebo controlled/ 12 week	10 mg tablet	Adults with nausea and/or vertigo of more than 5 days duration	19-Feb-2004 110	23/110	10 mg tablet: 21/57 Placebo: 22/53
A-005 Phase III Complete	Mexico, South Africa, Canada, France	Qweasytrol in the Treatment of Nausea and Vomiting Associated with Gastrointestinal Disorders and Chemotherapy	Random-ized, double blind, placebo controlled/ 52 week	10 mg tablet, 2 mg IV	Adults with nausea and/or vomiting of more than 10 days duration associated with chemotherapy or non-parasitic gastrointestinal disease	3-Mar-2004 2880	465/2786	10 mg tablet: 171/1088 Placebo tablet: 170/1080 2 mg IV: 62/317 Placebo IV:62/301
A-006 Phase II Ongoing	UK, Mexico	Safety & Efficacy of Qweasytrol in the Prevention of Vomiting Associated with Motion Sickness	Random-ized, double blind, placebo controlled/ 20 week	qweasytrol 10 mg tablet, diphenhydr-amine 25 mg tablet, meto-clopramide 10 mg tablet, placebo tablet	Adult subjects	22-Oct-2005 300	212/212	Study currently blinded. Estimate based on 1:1:1:1 randomization scheme: qweasytrol 10 mg tablet: 53/53

Study ID Phase Status	Countries	Trial Title	Design/ Treatment Duration	Dose & Regimen Control Therapy	Trial Population	First Visit First Patient & Planned Enrolment	Interval/ Cumulative Enrolment	Interval/ Cumulative Patient Exposure per Treatment Arm
								diphenhydramine 25 mg tablet: 53/53 metoclopramide 10 mg tablet: 53/53 placebo tablet: 53/53
A-007 Phase III Ongoing	UK, USA, Mexico, South Africa	Qweasytrol in the Symptomatic Treatment of Nausea and Vertigo Associated with Ménières Disease	Randomized, double blind, placebo controlled/ 20 week	qweasytrol 10 mg tablet & 2 mg IV, diphenhydr-amine 25 mg tablet, metoclo-pramide 10 mg tablet, placebo tablet & inj	Adult patients with docu-mented Ménières Disease	17-Dec-2005 1264	388/388	Study currently blinded. Estimate based on 1:1:1:1 randomization scheme: qweasytrol 10 mg tablet: 48/48 qweasytrol 2 mg IV: 49/49 diphenhydramine 25 mg tablet: 7/97 metoclopramide 10 mg tablet: 97/97 placebo tablet:49/49 placebo inj:48/48

Study ID Phase Status	Countries	Trial Title	Design/ Treatment Duration	Dose & Regimen Control Therapy	Trial Population	First Visit First Patient & Planned Enrolment	Interval/ Cumulative Enrolment	Interval/ Cumulative Patient Exposure per Treatment Arm
A-008 Phase III Ongoing	UK, Mexico	Qweasytrol in the Treatment of Nausea and Vomiting Associated with Cytotoxic Chemotherapy	Random-ized, double blind, placebo controlled/ 20 week	qweasytrol 10 mg tablet or 2 mg IV injection, diphenhydr-amine 25 mg tablet, meto-clopramide 10 mg tablet, placebo tablet & inj	Adults with nausea and/or vomiting of more than 10 days duration associated with	30-Sep-2005 2498	504/776	Study currently blinded. Estimate based on 1:1:1:1 randomization scheme. qweasytrol 10 mg tablet: 63/97 qweasytrol 2 mg IV injection: 63/97 diphenhydramine 25 mg tablet: 126/194 metoclopramide 10 mg tablet: 126/194 placebo tablet: 63/97 placebo inj: 63/97

Study ID Phase Status	Countries	Trial Title	Design/ Treatment Duration	Dose & Regimen Control Therapy	Trial Population	First Visit First Patient & Planned Enrolment	Interval/ Cumulative Enrolment	Interval/ Cumulative Patient Exposure per Treatment Arm
SAB-219 Phase II Ongoing	South Africa	Qweasytrol for the Prophylaxis of Acute Neurological Attacks in Patients with Porphyria Variegate	Random-ized, double blind, placebo controlled/ 1 week	400 mg tablet vs. placebo	Adult patients with documented porphyria variegate	23-Mar-2006 450	86/86	Study currently blinded. Estimate based on 1:1 randomization scheme. 400 mg tablet: 43/43 Placebo: 43/43
A-009 Phase IV Authorized	Mexico	Qweasytrol in the Treatment of Nausea and Vomiting due to Cytotoxic Chemotherapy	Observational postmarketing safety surveillance study/ 20 week	10 mg tablet	Large managed care organiza-tion patients and database	5000	0/0	0/0
TOTAL						**12645**	**1832/ 4568**	

Appendix B

Development Core Safety Information Available at Beginning of Report Period

Version number:	4
Version date:	08-Jul-2005
Date last updated version during review period:	24-May-2006
Version number latest version:	5

[Note to reader: no DCSI was prepared for this fictitious example.]

Appendix C

Line Listings

1. Qweasytrol

Reports Received by Andson Research Ltd. from 14-Jul-2005 to 13-Jul-2006 that Contain at Least One Suspected Unexpected Serious Adverse Reaction (SUSAR)* or ADR of Special Interest†

Company Reference Number	Country	Study Code (protocol)	Age (year)	Sex	Total Daily Dose & Route	Treatment Duration (days)	Ser	DR	MedDRA Preferred Term* †	Out-come #	Comment
MedDRA SOC											
Eye disorders											
S2754	South Africa	SAB-219	35	F	400 mg po	5	Y	Y	Vision blurred†	1	Qweasytrol discontinued
Hepatobiliary disorders											
AR-102856	Canada	A-005	27	F	10 mg po	25	Y N	Y U	Hepatitis* Headache	1 1	Concomitant HCTZ

Company Reference Number	Country	Study Code (protocol)	Age (year)	Sex	Total Daily Dose & Route	Treatment Duration (days)	Ser	DR	MedDRA Preferred Term* †	Out-come #	Comment
AR-101454	Mexico	A-006	65	M	10 mg po	31	Y	Y	Alanine amino-transferase abnormal*	1	Resolved while qweasytrol continued
AR-101667	Mexico	A-006	47	F	10 mg po	27	Y N	Y N	Aspartate ami-notransferase abnormal* Epigastric discomfort	1 1	Suspected excessive alcohol intake
Renal and urinary disorders											
AR-101594	Canada	A-005	67	M	10 mg po	58	Y N	Y N	Renal insufficiency* Syncope	4 1	Self-medica-tion with unspecified herbal medication
AR-102001	Canada	A-005	23	M	10 mg po	74	Y	Y	Renal insufficiency*	1	Qweasytrol discontinued
Skin and subcutaneous tissue disorders											
AR-101688	France	A-005	27	M	10 mg po	68	Y	Y	Urticaria*	1	Recent respiratory infection

Company Reference Number	Country	Study Code (protocol)	Age (year)	Sex	Total Daily Dose & Route	Treatment Duration (days)	Ser	DR	MedDRA Preferred Term* †	Out-come #	Comment
AR-101598	Mexico	A-005	52	M	10 mg po	32	Y N	Y N	<u>Urticaria</u>* Epigastric pain	1 1	History of drug allergy
AR-101632	South Africa	A-007	34	F	10 mg po	43	Y	Y	Urticaria*	1	History of urticaria

Ser = serious (Y – yes, N – no, U – unknown)
DR = drug-relationship (Y – yes, N – no, U – unknown)
* = SUSAR term
† = ADR of Special Interest
# = 1 – recovered, 2 – recovered with sequelae, 3 – not recovered, 4 – recovering, 5 – fatal, 6 – unknown

2. Metoclopramide

Reports Received by Andson Research Ltd. from 14-Jul-2005 to 13-Jul-2006 that Contain at Least One Suspected Unexpected Serious Adverse Reaction (SUSAR)* or ADR of Special Interest†

Company Reference Number	Country	Study Code (protocol)	Age	Sex	Total Daily Dose & Route	Treatment Duration (days)	Ser	DR	MedDRA Preferred Term* †	Out-come #	Comment
MedDRA SOC											
Blood and lymphatic system disorders											
AR-103766	UK	A-007	71	M	10 mg po	64	Y	Y	Leukopenia*	1	
AR-102575	UK	A-007	58	F	10 mg po	48	Y	Y	Leukopenia*	4	
Hepatobiliary disorders											
AR-100471	UK	A-007	45	F	10 mg po	24	Y N	Y U	Alanine aminotransferase abnormal* Diarrhoea	4 1	hypertension
Psychiatric disorders											

Company Reference Number	Country	Study Code (protocol)	Age	Sex	Total Daily Dose & Route	Treatment Duration (days)	Ser	DR	MedDRA Preferred Term* †	Out-come #	Comment
AR-104997	Mexico	A-007	24	F	10 mg po	5	Y	Y	Depression*	1	Resolved while continu-ing study treatment
AR-102111	UK	A-007	56	F	10 mg po	25	Y N	Y N	Confusional state* Headache	4 1	
Respiratory, thoracic and mediastinal disorders											
AR-104587	UK	A-006	32	M	10 mg po	12	Y	Y	Throat irritation*	4	Treatment discontinued
Skin and subcutaneous tissue disorders											
AR-102337	Mexico	A-007	47	M	10 mg po	23	Y	Y	Rash*	1	Concurrent unspecified OTC medication
AR-102734	UK	A-006	75	F	10 mg po	43	Y N	Y N	Rash* Disorientation	4 1	

Ser = serious (Y – yes, N – no, U – unknown)
DR = drug-relationship (Y – yes, N – no, U – unknown)
* = SUSAR term
† = ADR of Special Interest
# = 1 – recovered, 2 – recovered with sequelae, 3 – not recovered, 4 – recovering, 5 – fatal, 6 – unknown

Appendix C (continued)

3. Diphenhydramine

Reports Received by Andson Research Ltd. from 14-Jul-2005 to 13-Jul-2006 that Contain at Least One Suspected Unexpected Serious Adverse Reaction (SUSAR)* or ADR of Special Interest†

Company Reference Number	Country	Study Code (protocol)	Age	Sex	Total Daily Dose & Route	Treatment Duration (days)	Ser	DR	MedDRA Preferred Term* †	Out-come #	Comment
MedDRA SOC											
General disorders and administration site conditions											
AR-100571	UK	A-006	35	M	25 mg po	44	Y N	Y N	Gait disturbance* Headache	1 1	
Nervous system disorders											
AR-101469	UK	A-006	37	M	25 mg po	12	Y	Y	Syncope*	1	Concurrent hypertension
Renal and urinary disorders											
AR-103274	Mexico	A-007	72	F	25 mg po	67	Y Y	Y N	Haematuria* Epigastric discomfort	1 1	

Ser = serious (Y – yes, N – no, U – unknown)
DR = drug-relationship (Y – yes, N – no, U – unknown)
* = SUSAR term
† = ADR of Special Interest
# = 1 – recovered, 2 – recovered with sequelae, 3 – not recovered, 4 – recovering, 5 – fatal, 6 – unknown

Appendix D

Cumulative Summary Tabulation of Serious Adverse Events, Including Adverse Events of Special Interest, for the Period from 14-Jul-2002 to 13-Jul-2006 for All Indications and Dosage Forms

(Due to the interim nature of these data, this tabulation may include data from ongoing clinical trials which may not have been reconciled.)

MedDRA System Organ Class (SOC)	MedDRA Preferred Term	Qweasytrol	Placebo	Metoclo-pramide	Diphen-hydramine	Blinded	Grand Total
Blood and lymphatic system disorders	Haemolytic anemia					2	**2**
	Leukopenia			**2**			**2**
SOC TOTAL		0	0	2	0	2	**4**
Cardiac disorders	Angina pectoris		1				**1**
	Palpitations		1				**1**
	Tachycardia					2	**2**
SOC TOTAL		0	2	0	0	2	**4**
Ear and labyrinth disorders	Tinnitus					1	**1**
SOC TOTAL		0	0	0	0	1	**1**
Eye disorders	Vision blurred†	**1**	**1**				**2**
SOC TOTAL		1	1	0	0	0	**2**
Gastrointestinal disorders	Epigastric discomfort	**1**			**1**		**2**

MedDRA System Organ Class (SOC)	MedDRA Preferred Term	Qweasytrol	Placebo	Metoclo-pramide	Diphen-hydramine	Blinded	Grand Total
SOC TOTAL		1	0	0	1	0	**2**
General disorders and administration site conditions	Gait disturbance				**1**	2	**3**
SOC TOTAL		0	0	0	1	2	**3**
Hepatobiliary disorders	Hepatitis*	**1**					**1**
SOC TOTAL		1	0	0	0	0	**1**
Immune system disorders	Hypersensitivity	1			2	2	**5**
SOC TOTAL		1	0	0	2	2	**5**
Infections and infestations	Bronchitis			1			**1**
	Infection			1		2	**3**
SOC TOTAL		0	0	2	0	2	**4**
Injury, poisoning and procedural complications	Overdose	**4**		1	1		**6**
	Drug exposure during pregnancy	1					**1**
SOC TOTAL		5	0	1	1		**7**

MedDRA System Organ Class (SOC)	MedDRA Preferred Term	Qweasytrol	Placebo	Metoclo-pramide	Diphen-hydramine	Blinded	Grand Total
Investigations	Alanine aminotransferase abnormal*	**1**		**1**		3	**5**
	Aspartate aminotransferase abnormal*	**1**			1	2	**4**
	Blood creatine phosphokinase abnormal			1		1	**2**
SOC TOTAL		2	0	2	1	6	**11**
Metabolism and nutrition disorders	Fluid retention		1				**1**
	Hyperlipidaemia				2		**2**
	Metabolic disorder			2			**2**
SOC TOTAL		0	1	2	2	0	**5**
Musculoskeletal and connective tissue disorders	Back pain		1				**1**
SOC TOTAL		0	1	0	0	0	**1**
Nervous system disorders	Syncope	**1**			**1**		**2**
SOC TOTAL		1	0	0	1	0	**2**
Psychiatric discrders	Confusional state			**1**		1	**2**
	Depression			**1**		2	**3**
	Disorientation			**1**			**1**

MedDRA System Organ Class (SOC)	MedDRA Preferred Term	Qweasytrol	Placebo	Metoclo-pramide	Diphen-hydramine	Blinded	Grand Total
SOC TOTAL		0	0	3	0	3	**6**
Renal and urinary disorders	Renal insufficiency*	**18**	**8**				**26**
	Haematuria		**1**		**1**		**2**
SOC TOTAL		18	9	0	1	0	**28**
Respiratory, thoracic and mediastinal disorders	Throat irritation			**1**		1	**2**
SOC TOTAL		0	0	1	0	1	**2**
Skin and subcutaneous tis-sue disorders	Rash	**0**		**2**			**2**
	Urticaria*	**3**	**1**				**4**
SOC TOTAL		5	1	2	0	0	**8**
Vascular disorders	Hypertension					2	**2**
SOC TOTAL		0	0	0	0	2	**2**
Grand Total		**35**	**15**	**15**	**10**	**23**	**97**

* = SUSAR term
† = AE of Special Interest

Appendix E

1. Cumulative Summary Tabulation of Serious Adverse Events, Including Adverse Events of Special Interest, for the Period from 14-Jul-2002 to 13-Jul-2006 by All Indications Except Porphyria Variegate

(Due to the interim nature of these data, this tabulation may include data from ongoing clinical trials which may not have been reconciled.)

		Motion Sickness, Ménières Disease, Gastrointestinal Disorders, Cytotoxic Chemotherapy					
MedDRA System Organ Class (SOC)	**MedDRA Preferred Term**	**Qweasytrol**	**Placebo**	**Metoclo-pramide**	**Diphen-hydramine**	**Blinded**	**Grand Total**
Blood and lymphatic system disorders	Haemolytic anemia					2	**2**
	Leukopenia			**2**			**2**
SOC TOTAL		0	0	2	0	2	**4**
Cardiac disorders	Angina pectoris		1				**1**
	Palpitations		1				**1**
	Tachycardia					2	**2**
SOC TOTAL		0	2	0	0	2	**4**
Eye disorders	Vision blurred†		**1**				**1**
SOC TOTAL		0	1	0	0	0	**2**

		Motion Sickness, Ménières Disease, Gastrointestinal Disorders, Cytotoxic Chemotherapy					
MedDRA System Organ Class (SOC)	**MedDRA Preferred Term**	**Qweasytrol**	**Placebo**	**Metoclo-pramide**	**Diphen-hydramine**	**Blinded**	**Grand Total**
Gastrointestinal disorders	Epigastric discomfort	**1**			**1**		**2**
SOC TOTAL		1	0	0	1	0	**2**
General disorders and ad-ministration site conditions	Gait disturbance				**1**	2	**3**
SOC TOTAL		0	0	0	1	2	**3**
Hepatobiliary disorders	Hepatitis*	**1**					**1**
SOC TOTAL		1	0	0	0	0	**1**
Immune system disorders	Hypersensitivity	1			2	2	**5**
SOC TOTAL		1	0	0	2	2	**5**
Infections and infestations	Bronchitis			1			**1**
	Infection			1		2	**3**
SOC TOTAL		0	0	2	0	2	**4**
Injury, poisoning and procedural complications	Overdose	**4**		1	1		**6**
	Drug exposure during pregnancy	1					**1**
SOC TOTAL		5	0	1	1		**7**

		Motion Sickness, Ménières Disease, Gastrointestinal Disorders, Cytotoxic Chemotherapy					
MedDRA System Organ Class (SOC)	**MedDRA Preferred Term**	**Qweasytrol**	**Placebo**	**Metoclo-pramide**	**Diphen-hydramine**	**Blinded**	**Grand Total**
Investigations	Alanine aminotransferase abnormal*	**1**		**1**		3	**5**
	Aspartate aminotransferase abnormal*	**1**			1	2	**4**
	Blood creatine phosphokinase abnormal			1		1	**2**
SOC TOTAL		2	0	2	1	6	**11**
Metabolism and nutrition disorders	Fluid retention		1				**1**
	Hyperlipidaemia				2		**2**
	Metabolic disorder			2			**2**
SOC TOTAL		0	1	2	2	0	**5**
Musculoskeletal and connective tissue disorders	Back pain		1				**1**
SOC TOTAL		0	1	0	0	0	**1**
Nervous system disorders	Syncope	**1**			**1**		**2**

		Motion Sickness, Ménières Disease, Gastrointestinal Disorders, Cytotoxic Chemotherapy					
MedDRA System Organ Class (SOC)	**MedDRA Preferred Term**	**Qweasytrol**	**Placebo**	**Metoclo-pramide**	**Diphen-hydramine**	**Blinded**	**Grand Total**
Psychiatric disorders	Confusional state			**1**		1	**2**
	Depression			**1**		2	**3**
	Disorientation			**1**			**1**
SOC TOTAL		0	0	3	0	3	**6**
Renal and urinary disorders	Renal insufficiency*	**18**	**8**				**26**
	Haematuria		**1**		**1**		**2**
SOC TOTAL		18	9	0	1	0	**28**
Respiratory, thoracic and mediastinal disorders	Throat irritation			**1**		1	**2**
SOC TOTAL		0	0	1	0	1	**2**
Skin and subcutaneous tissue disorders	Rash	**0**		**2**			**2**
	Urticaria*	**3**	**1**				**4**
SOC TOTAL		5	1	2	0	0	**8**
Vascular disorders	Hypertension					2	**2**
SOC TOTAL		0	0	0	0	2	**2**
GRAND TOTAL		**34**	**15**	**15**	**10**	**20**	**93**

* = SUSAR term
† = AE of Special Interest

Appendix E (continued)

2. Cumulative Summary Tabulation of Serious Adverse Events, Including Adverse Events of Special Interest, for the Period from 14-Jul-2002 to 13-Jul-2006 for the Indicaiton Porphyria Variegate

(Due to the interim nature of these data, this tabulation may include data from ongoing clinical trials which may not have been reconciled.)

MedDRA System Organ Class (SOC)	MedDRA Preferred Term	Qweasytrol	Placebo	Blinded	Grand Total
Ear and labyrinth disorders	Tinnitus			1	**1**
SOC TOTAL		0	0	1	**1**
Eye disorders	Vision blurred†	**1**			**1**
SOC TOTAL		1	0	0	**1**
Vascular disorders	Hypertension			2	**2**
SOC TOTAL		0	0	2	**2**
GRAND TOTAL		**1**	**0**	**3**	**4**

* = SUSAR term
† = AE of Special Interest

Appendix F

Cumulative Summary Tabulation of Serious Adverse Events, Including Adverse Events of Special Interest, for the Period from 14-Jul-2002 to 13-Jul-2006 by Formulation

(Due to the interim nature of these data, this tabulation may include data from ongoing clinical trials which may not have been reconciled.)

		TABLET						INJECTION			
MedDRA System Organ Class (SOC)	MedDRA Preferred Term	Qweasytrol	Placebo	Metoclopramide	Diphenhydramine	Blinded	Grand Total	Qweasytrol	Placebo	Blinded	Grand Total
Blood and lymphatic system disorders	Haemolytic anemia					2	2				
	Leukopenia			2			2				
SOC TOTAL		0	0	2	0	2	4	0	0	0	0
Cardiac disorders	Angina pectoris								1		1
	Palpitations		1				1				
	Tachycardia					1	1			1	1

		TABLET						INJECTION			
MedDRA System Organ Class (SOC)	MedDRA Preferred Term	Qweasytrol	Placebo	Metoclopramide	Diphenhydramine	Blinded	Grand Total	Qweasytrol	Placebo	Blinded	Grand Total
SOC TOTAL		0	1	0	0	1	2	0	1	1	2
Ear and labyrinth disorders	Tinnitus					1	1				
SOC TOTAL		0	0	0	0	1	1	0	0	0	0
Eye disorders	Vision blurred†	1	1				2				
SOC TOTAL		1	1	0	0	0	2	0	0	0	0
Gastrointestinal disorders	Epigastric discomfort	1			1		2				
SOC TOTAL		1	0	0	1	0	2	0	0	0	0
General disorders and administration site conditions	Gait disturbance				1	1	2			1	1
SOC TOTAL		0	0	0	1	1	2	0	0	1	1
Hepatobiliary disorders	Hepatitis*	1					1				
SOC TOTAL		1	0	0	0	0	1	0	0	0	0
Immune system disorders	Hypersensitivity	1			2	2	5				
SOC TOTAL		1	0	0	2	2	5	0	0	0	0
Infections and infestations	Bronchitis			1			1				
	Infection			1		1	2			1	1

MedDRA System Organ Class (SOC)	MedDRA Preferred Term	TABLET						INJECTION			
		Qweasytrol	Placebo	Metoclopramide	Diphenhydramine	Blinded	Grand Total	Qweasytrol	Placebo	Blinded	Grand Total
SOC TOTAL		0	0	2	0	1	3	0	0	1	1
Injury, poisoning and procedural complications	Overdose	4		1	1		6				
	Drug exposure during pregnancy	1					1				
SOC TOTAL		5	0	1	1	0	7	0	0	0	0
Investigations	Alanine aminotransferase abnormal*	1		1		3	5				
	Aspartate aminotransferase abnormal*	1			1	2	4				
	Blood creatine phosphokinase abnormal			1		1	2				
SOC TOTAL		2	0	2	1	6	11	0	0	0	0
Metabolism and nutrition disorders	Fluid retention		1				1				
	Hyperlipidaemia				2		2				
	Metabolic disorder			2			2				
SOC TOTAL		0	1	2	2	0	5	0	0	0	0
Musculoskeletal and connective tissue disorders	Back pain		1				1				

MedDRA System Organ Class (SOC)	MedDRA Preferred Term	TABLET						INJECTION			
		Qweasytrol	Placebo	Metoclopramide	Diphenhydramine	Blinded	Grand Total	Qweasytrol	Placebo	Blinded	Grand Total
SOC TOTAL		0	1	0	0	0	1	0	0	0	0
Nervous system disorders	Syncope	1			1		2				
SOC TOTAL		1	0	0	1	0	2	0	0	0	0
Psychiatric disorders	Confusional state			1		1	2				
	Depression			1		2	3				
	Disorientation			1			1				
SOC TOTAL		0	0	3	0	3	6	0	0	0	0
Renal and urinary disorders	Renal insufficiency*	18	8				26				
	Haematuria		1		1		2				
SOC TOTAL		18	9	0	1	0	28	0	0	0	0
Respiratory, thoracic and mediastinal disorders	Throat irritation			1		1	2				
SOC TOTAL		0	0	1	0	1	2	0	0	0	0
Skin and subcutaneous tissue disorders	Rash	0		2			2				
	Urticaria*	3	1				4				
SOC TOTAL		5	1	2	0	0	8	0	0	0	0
Vascular disorders	Hypertension					2	2				
SOC TOTAL		0	0	0	0	2	2	0	0	0	0
GRAND TOTAL		**35**	**14**	**15**	**10**	**20**	**95**	**0**	**1**	**3**	**4**

* = SUSAR term
† = AE of Special Interest

B. Sample DSUR for a Non-Commercial Investigator

DEVELOPMENT SAFETY UPDATE REPORT #2

Drug:	GAGF-1
Sponsor:	Dr. First M. Last General Hospital, Major University 123 Main Street Room 101 Anytown, TX, 12345-1234 USA
Review period:	17 Feb 2007 – 16 Feb 2008
Development International Birth Date:	17 Feb 2006
Date of the report:	2 Apr 2008

Note: This Developmental Safety Update Report contains information that is confidential and proprietary.

Table of Contents

Appendices to DSUR

Appendix A: Inventory of Ongoing and Completed Interventional Clinical Trials
Appendix B: Safety Sections of IB Available at Beginning of Report Period
Appendix C: Line Listing(s)
Appendix D: Cumulative Summary Tabulation

Executive Summary

Grandiose Angiogenic Growth Factor-1 (GAGF-1) is an angiogenic, heparin-binding, 29-kD polypeptide growth factor belonging to the ABC super-family. GAGF-1 is under development for the treatment of angina pectoris in patients with coronary artery disease by DrugCompany, Corp.

Our Department has studied the potential salutary effects of GAGF-1 in peripheral arterial disease (PAD). In a rabbit model of PAD (unilateral femoral artery ligation), we showed that a single dose of GAGF-1 enhanced arteriogenesis, limb perfusion, and limb survival. Thus, we embarked on a Phase II trial of GAGF-1 in subjects with symptomatic PAD: "GAGF-1 as Angiogenic TheRapy for Symptomatic PEripheral VAscular Disease, a Phase II STudy: 'GREAT.'" The primary study objective is to evaluate the safety, tolerability, and pharmacokinetics of GAGF-1 in the PAD population. As a secondary objective, we seek to gain some evidence of biological activity (as assessed by exercise capacity).

Safety:

Based on data from DrugCompany, the main safety concerns of GAGF-1 are acute hypotension, proteinuria, and anemia. The hypotensive effects are thought to be mediated by NO-dependent vasodilatation; the mechanisms responsible for proteinuria and anemia are unknown at this time. Additional concerns regarding this angiogenic polypeptide relate to its potential to cause exaggerated or uncontrolled neovascularization. The potential for retinal neovascularization and promotion of tumor development are specific concerns related to this product. To date, we are not aware of cases of retinal neovascularization or tumor promotion in DrugCompany's coronary artery disease studies (completed Phase I and Phase II studies; ongoing Phase III study). In our study, retinal photography has been negative in all subjects who have undergone Week 24 follow-up, and none of the subjects has experienced a new tumor.

There has also been some concern regarding GAGF-1's potential for hepatic toxicity. This concern has, as its basis, findings in a rat toxicology study, where rats exposed to repeated high doses of GAGF-1 (500 mg/kg X 14 days) developed hepatic toxicity (acute, non-cholestatic, cytokine-mediated liver injury). In our ongoing study, planned exposure is considerably less than this. Subjects are receiving only a single dose of GAGF-1 (or placebo), and the highest dose planned is 30 mg/kg. Thus, there appears to be an adequate safety margin. Nevertheless, one subject in the 3 mg/kg cohort was hospitalized for asymptomatic acute liver injury, two weeks after receiving a single dose of GAGF-1. Transaminases eventually peaked at approximately 15X the upper limit of normal, with small increases in bilirubin and alkaline phosphatase. The history was confounded by the fact that the subject had been receiving concomitant drugs "X," "Y," and "Z," and drug "Y" is known to be hepatotoxic. Drugs "X," "Y," and "Z" were withdrawn, and transaminases, bilirubin, and alkaline phosphatase returned to normal after three months. Although transaminase elevations are not uncommon with drug "Y," the subject had been receiving drug "Y" for approximately two years without problems, and the temporal relation between GAGF-1 administration and hepatic injury suggests a causal effect. Therefore, the protocol was revised to exclude potential subjects with a history of hepatic disease, and to provide more intensive monitoring of liver function. In addition, the Investigators Brochure and Informed Consent documents were revised to highlight the events and findings in this subject.

We are not aware of any other important safety issues that have arisen during this DSUR reporting period.

Given the stage of development of the product, the risks still seem acceptable, especially when considered in light of the serious morbidity of peripheral vascular disease, and the promise of this angiogenic therapy to ameliorate symptoms. Moreover, by excluding potential subjects with a background history of hepatic disease, and by monitoring transaminases more frequently, we feel that we should be able to detect hepatic transaminase elevations at an earlier stage, at a time when they are reversible.

1. Introduction

This is the second Development Safety Update Report (DSUR) for Great Angiogenic Growth Factor-1 (GAGF-1), covering the period from 17 Feb 2007 to 16 Feb 2008.

GAGF-1 is a biotechnology-derived product, an angiogenic, heparin-binding 29-kD polypeptide growth factor belonging to the ABC superfamily. GAGF-1 has been shown to promote coronary collateral development in a number of animal models of single-vessel coronary artery disease, and is under development for the treatment of angina pectoris in patients with coronary artery disease by DrugCompany, Corp., Anytown, USA (letter of cross-reference provided with original IND submission). GAGF-1 is supplied as a lyophilized powder (1000 mg/vial) that is reconstituted in sterile water prior to intravenous injection. The product used in this study is supplied to us by DrugCompany, and is identical to the product being evaluated in studies in coronary artery disease.

Our laboratory has shown that GAGF-1 promotes collateral development in a rabbit hindlimb model of PAD (Last FM, et. al., *J Adv Med Ther*. 2004; 36:1239). The mechanism of action is thought to involve arteriogenesis, although this has not been definitely established. For further details, see the Investigators Brochure (latest version [revision 2] was submitted in IND amendment 0014).

The objective of the study is to evaluate the safety, tolerability, and pharmacokinetics of GAGF-1 in the PAD population, and to gain some evidence of biological activity.

This DSUR covers our single phase 2 trial of GAGF-1 in subjects with symptomatic peripheral arterial disease (PAD). We have provided a copy of this report to DrugCompany, Corp.

2. Worldwide Marketing Authorization Status

To our knowledge, GAGF-1 has not been granted marketing approval in the US or elsewhere, but is under study for coronary artery disease by DrugCompany, Corp., as noted above.

3. Update on Actions Taken for Safety Reasons

One subject enrolled in the trial, subject 108, was hospitalized for acute hepatic injury on 12 December 2007 (see details under 7, below). This event was considered by the General Hospital Institutional Review Board at their 15 Jan 2008 meeting. In light of the pre-clinical data, demonstrating hepatic injury at higher doses, the protocol was revised, as follows:

The following potential subjects will now be excluded from study participation (HIV positive patients continue to be excluded):

- prior history of hepatitis;
- transaminases (aspartate aminotransferase [AST], alanine aminotransferase [ALT], or gamma glutamyl transpeptidase [GGTP]) above upper limit of normal for local laboratory;
- positive serology for hepatitis A, B, or C.

Originally, subjects were to have liver function studies assessed at screening, Week 12, and Week 24 (or at the time of premature discontinuation). In light of the adverse event in subject 108, subjects will now undergo more frequent tests of hepatic function (ALT, AST, GGTP, alkaline phosphatase, LDH, and direct and indirect bilirubin). Specifically, in addition to undergoing these tests at screening, Weeks 12 and 24, subjects will also be tested at Weeks 1, 2, 4, 6, and 18.

The consent form has been revised, as follows (under "risks of participation," page 4):

"Your participation in this study carries with it a risk of liver damage. In a rat study conducted by DrugCompany, the discoverer of GAGF-1, there was evidence of liver injury with doses of GAGF-1 about 15-times higher than the highest dose you might receive as a participant in this study. One patient in this study who received GAGF-1 (195 mg) developed a liver problem 2 weeks after his dose was given. It is not clear if the liver problem was directly related to the drug. Nevertheless, you should be aware that there is a potential risk of liver damage with this drug. We will test your blood for liver problems before you participate in the study, and we will re-check your blood for evidence of liver damage 1, 2, 4, 6, 12, 18 and 24 weeks after you receive GAGF-1 or salt water (placebo)."

Page 5:

"The total amount of blood required over 24 weeks will be about nine ounces (270 mL)."

No other actions have been taken for safety reasons during the period of this DSUR.

4. Changes to Reference Safety Information

Based on the above event, the safety section of the Investigator Brochure (IB) has been revised; a copy of the new version will be submitted shortly to the Agency.

5. Inventory and Status of Ongoing and Completed Interventional Clinical Trials

The only study covered by this DSUR is: "GAGF-1 as Angiogenic TheRapy for Symptomatic PEripheral VAscular Disease, a Phase II STudy: 'GREAT.'" The primary objectives of this Phase II study are to evaluate the safety, tolerability, and pharmacokinetics of GAGF-1 in the PAD population. As a secondary goal, we hope to gain some evidence of biological activity by assessing the effect of GAGF-1 on six-minute walk (6-MW) distance. The study is being conducted at a single site (General Hospital, Major University). The conduct of this trial was authorised by the FDA on 21 Jun 2006 (BB-IND 00000).

"GREAT" is a double-blind, placebo-controlled, serial, dose-escalation study. We plan to enroll 32 subjects (8 per dosing cohort). Sequential cohorts are planned to receive a single dose of 1, 3, 10, or 30 mg/kg GAGF-1, or placebo, as follows:

Cohort 1:	GAGF-1, 1 mg/kg;	or placebo	(n = 8; randomized 3:1)
Cohort 2:	GAGF-1, 3 mg/kg;	or placebo	(n = 8; randomized 3:1)
Cohort 3:	GAGF-1, 10 mg/kg;	or placebo	(n = 8; randomized 3:1)
Cohort 4:	GAGF-1, 30 mg/kg;	or placebo	(n = 8; randomized 3:1)

In total, 24 subjects are planned to receive GAGF-1; 8 are planned to receive placebo. All subjects are to be monitored through 24 weeks. Fixed-block randomization is used, with a block size of 4.

Male and female subjects, age ≥18, with symptomatic PAD are being enrolled.

The First Visit for the First Patient (FVFP) was 25 Aug 2006.

Status: As of 16 Feb 2008, 17 subjects have been enrolled (~1 subject per month). The first two dosing cohorts have been completed (1 and 3 mg/kg), and one subject has been enrolled in the third dosing cohort (10 mg/kg).

6. Estimated Patient Exposure in Clinical Trials

Of note, this study is still blinded; the numbers provided are based on the randomization scheme:

Subject exposure through 16 Feb 2008:

1 mg/kg	➔ n = 6
3 mg/kg	➔ n = 6
10 mg/kg	➔ n = 0 or 1
placebo	➔ n = 4 or 5

7. Presentation of Safety Data from the Clinical Study "GREAT"

Serious Adverse Events:

a. Subject 104 is a 62 year-old female who experienced transient unilateral visual loss on 8 Jan 2008, 5 months after receiving GAGF-1, 1 mg/kg (79 mg) IV. (Treatment assignment for this subject was unblinded.) The visual loss was attributed to central retinal artery occlusion, which was thought to be embolic in nature. The patient had a history of paroxysmal atrial fibrillation, and non-compliance with warfarin. A transthoracic echocardiogram showed evidence of left atrial thrombus, one day after the event.

b. Subject 108 is a 59 year-old male who was hospitalized for asymptomatic, acute hepatic injury on 12 Dec 2007. His treatment assignment was unblinded, per protocol, and it was determined that he had received 195 mg GAGF-1 (3 mg/kg) on 28 Nov 2007. Concomitant medications included drugs "X," "Y," and "Z." All drugs were discontinued on 14 Dec 2007. Ultrasound was negative for obstruction; liver biopsy was considered, but the patient refused this, and he was discharged on 15 Dec 2007. Transaminases peaked at 15-times the upper limit of normal on 29 Dec 2007 and declined thereafter. Bilirubin and alkaline phosphatase were minimally elevated; prothrombin time was not elevated. All relevant serology studies were negative. The subject was seen in consultation by the Liver Service. They believed that Drug "Y" provided a plausible cause for the transaminase elevations; however, they noted that drug "Y" does not typically cause transaminase elevations of this magnitude, and the patient had been on drug "Y" for approximately two years without known problems. Thus, in light of the magnitude of the transaminase elevations, the negative serology for infectious causes of hepatitis, and most importantly, the temporal association with GAGF-1 administration, the consultants were concerned about the role of GAGF-1 in causing hepatotoxicity in this subject. By 26 Feb 2008, all liver function tests had returned to normal. Ultimately, drugs "X" and "Z" were restarted. Given the potential hepatotoxicity of drug "Y," it was not re-initiated, and the patient was switched to drug "A" for management of his dyslipidemia. Transaminase elevations have not been observed in other subjects in the study.

c. Subject 112 is a 63 year-old male who presented to his local emergency department on 16 Aug 2007 (25 days after treatment with GAGF-1,

3 mg/kg, or placebo) with critical limb ischemia of the left lower extremity. He was admitted to the hospital and stabilized with angioplasty, but subsequently required a below-the-knee amputation for ongoing ischemia. Vascular complications are part of the natural history of PAD, and, as agreed to by the FDA previously and per protocol, they are not being reported in expedited fashion. Treatment assignment was not unblinded for this subject, as agreed previously.

8. Significant Findings from Interventional Clinical Trials

Atrial fibrillation, retinal artery occlusion, and arterial embolism were not listed in the Investigator's Brochure (IB) at the beginning of the period, and are new concerns. Acute hepatitis was previously cited as a risk, based on the preclinical information. There is some likelihood that the hepatic injury SAE (subject 108, above) was related to GAGF-1. As a result of these concerns, the IB has been updated, additional monitoring is in place, and more stringent study entrance exclusions have been implemented.

9. Observational and Epidemiological Studies

Not applicable.

10. Other Information

(1) Lack of Efficacy: Not applicable.

(2) Chemistry, Manufacturing and Formulation Issues: Not applicable.

(3) Non-Clinical Findings: Not applicable.

(4) Literature: A review of MedLine citations, searched 31 Mar 2008, did not provide new information relevant to the safety of GAGF-1. MeSH headings included: "GAGF-1," "GAGF," "ABC," "Grandiose," and "Angiogenic Growth Factor." We are not aware of the publication or presentation of any abstracts during the reporting period relevant to the safety of GAGF-1.

11. Information from Marketing Experience

Not applicable.

12. Late Breaking Information

All pertinent information is included above.

13. Overall Safety Evaluation

a. Evaluation of the Risks

Overall, there is little new safety information to report since one year ago. Based on data from DrugCompany, Corp., GAGF-1's main safety concerns are acute hypotension, proteinuria, and anemia. On a theoretical basis, additional concerns regarding this angiogenic product relate to neovascularization, its putative mechanism of action. Specifically, retinal neovascularization and promotion of tumor development are concerns with this product. To date, none of these concerns has been borne out in our study (retinal photography has been negative, and there have been no tumors).

The potential for hepatic toxicity was previously highlighted in the Investigators Brochure and Informed Consent, based on the findings in study RAT-101. However, in light of the transaminase elevations in Subject 108 (see above), and their temporal relation to GAGF-1 administration, the protocol has been revised to include stricter inclusion criteria, and to implement more frequent monitoring for hepatic toxicity.

Thus, relative to our 2007 DSUR, there is more evidence in favor of GAGF-1-induced hepatic toxicity. Given that subjects receive only a single dose of GAGF-1, there can be no provision to re-challenge subjects, a tactic that might better define this risk.

b. Benefit-Risk Considerations

Given the stage of development of the product, the risks still seem acceptable, despite clearer evidence of a risk of serious hepatic injury. (It should also be noted that hepatic injury was reversible, and was not associated with important symptoms or complications.) Moreover, by excluding potential subjects with a background history of hepatic disease, and by monitoring transaminases more frequently, we believe that we should be able to detect hepatic transaminase elevations at an earlier stage, when they are reversible. The risks must be considered in light of the serious morbidity of peripheral vascular disease, and the theoretical potential of this angiogenic therapy – not only to ameliorate symptoms, but to salvage ischemic limbs as well.

14. Summary of Important Risks

1. Proteinuria. GAGF-1 was associated with proteinuria in Drug Company's Phase I and Phase II trials in coronary artery disease. We have no new information on this risk. To date, we have not observed new proteinuria, or worsening proteinuria, in our PAD subject population. We continue to monitor 24-hour urinary protein excretion at baseline, Weeks 2, 6, and 24.

2. Acute hypotension. Acute hypotension was observed in 23% of subjects in DrugCompany's completed coronary artery disease studies. This was mostly mild, and thought to be related to the rapidity of infusion. Based on this premise, the infusion rate in our study is approximately 25% the infusion rate in DrugCompany's coronary artery disease studies, and we have observed only mild, transient hypotension. One subject became transiently lightheaded, but the drop in blood pressure was minimal (4/9 mmHg). None of our subjects have required intravenous fluids or pharmacologic agents to support their blood pressure. When we are further into our highest dosing cohort (30 mg/kg), hypotension could become more of a problem. For now, we will continue to monitor subjects closely.

3. Anemia. Anemia has been associated with other growth factors of this class. The mechanism of action is unknown, but thought to be a direct bone marrow effect. We have observed mild decreases in hemoglobin in our study, with primarily normal RBC indices and low reticulocyte counts, although we remain blinded to treatment assignment. Of note, these subjects undergo frequent phlebotomy for laboratory tests, and the hemoglobin changes may be difficult to interpret. We will continue to monitor complete blood counts, and fully investigate any cases of anemia.

4. Hepatic toxicity. In study RAT101, 4 rats per cohort received 5, 15, 50, 150, and 500 mg/kg GAGF-1, given IV on a daily basis for two weeks. Three (3) of 4 rats in the 500 mg/kg group developed hepatic

injury, with centilobular necrosis. There is no clear evidence of hepatic toxicity from the coronary artery disease studies (based on communications with DrugCompany, transaminase elevations have been observed, but the rates with GAGF-1 and placebo have been approximately the same). One patient in "GREAT" who received 3 mg/kg GAGF-1 experienced hepatic transaminase elevations (see section 7, above). As a result, more judicious monitoring has been implemented in the protocol, and the consent form has been updated.

15. New Actions Recommended

No new actions are recommended. As noted, the protocol, Investigators Brochure and Informed Consent have been revised as a result of the subject with acute hepatic injury (see section 8). No other actions are planned at this time.

16. Conclusions

We conclude that the safety data remain fairly consistent with the experience described in our previous DSUR. We believe that the data obtained justify continuation of the development programme, with the changes noted above.

Appendix A

Inventory of Ongoing and Completed Interventional Clinical Trials

Study name:	"GREAT: GAGF-1 as Angiogenic TheRapy for Symptomatic PEripheral VAscular Disease, a Phase II STudy"
Formulation:	lyophilized powder (1000 mg/vial)
Indication:	Peripheral Arterial Disease (PAD)
Phase:	II
Status:	ongoing
Design:	randomized, double-blind, placebo-controlled, single ascending dose study
Treatment duration:	single dose
Dose and Regimen:	Subjects receive 1, 3, 10, or 30 mg/kg GAGF-1 or matching placebo
Subject population:	Patients with symptomatic PAD
First Visit First Patient:	5 Aug 2006
Planned Enrollment:	32 (24 active : 8 placebo control)
Interval Enrollment:	11 (roughly 8 : 3)
Cumulative Enrollment:	17 (roughly 13 : 4)

Appendix B

Development Core Safety Information or Safety Sections of Investigator Brochure (IB) Available at the Beginning of the Review Period

Version number:	1.2
Version date:	9 Aug 2006
Date last updated version during review period:	pending
Version number latest version:	1.3

Note to readers: A real DSUR would contain a copy of the DCSI or the safety sections of the IB in this appendix.

Appendix C

Suspected Unexpected Serious Adverse Reactions (SUSARs) in the "GREAT" Study

Subject Number	Age	Sex	Total Dose	Serious	Events	Outcome	Comment
104	62	F	1 mg/kg (79 mg) IV	Y	Vision blurred; arterial embolism; retinal artery occlusion	improved	History atrial fibrillation, warfarin non-compliance

Appendix D

Cumulative Summary Tabulation of Serious Adverse Events, 25 Aug 2006 to 16 Feb 2008

Event	Placebo	Study Drug	Blind Treatment	Total
Hospitalization for herniorrhaphy			1	1
Seizure			1	1
Acute hepatic injury		1		1
Vision blurred; arterial embolism; retinal artery occlusion		1		1
TOTAL		**2**	**2**	**4**

Appendix 5

Template for Clinical Study Synopsis

The following template is recommended for use in summarizing the salient results of completed clinical trials, or for ongoing trials for which an interim analysis has been conducted. It contains most of the items specified in ICH Guideline E3 (Structure and Content of Clinical Study Reports) for the Synopsis of a report, but without the unnecessary administrative information and with more focus on safety results. It is in the form of a checklist outline. Rather than incorporate the information into a typical summary narrative, for simplicity and brevity it is recommended that the information be succinctly stated next to each of the items listed. Not all the items will require inclusion or completion, depending on the particular study.

It is possible that many of the parameters listed could be incorporated into a summary table, which can be considered as an option, depending on the item.

Study Title: Will generally be the same as the title of the protocol as listed in Appendix A of the DSUR.

Clinical Study Type: Indicate whether Phase I, II, III or IV, or observational (non-interventional)

Study Status: Indicate whether completed or ongoing.

Study Rationale: Role of this particular study in the clinical development programme

Indication(s) Treated and Study Objective: the objective may be stated in the title in which case it need not be repeated here.

Number and Location(s) of Study Centres: Indicate how many sites and in which countries.

Study Design: Open or blinded; parallel or cross-over; comparative or non-comparative

Dosage Form/Formulation for Investigational Drug: capsule, tablet, iv, im, etc. Describe any special features that may pertain (e.g., slow release, special iv solution, etc.)

Investigational Drug: Dose, regimen, and mode of administration

Reference Therapy(ies): Dose, regimen, mode of administration

Number of Subjects: Provide the numbers planned, enrolled, and analysed for each treatment arm.

Demographics of Population: Provide summary statistics on the age, gender, and if relevant the ethnicity or racial characteristics of the study population.

Main Criteria for Inclusion: Not a comprehensive listing but only the key items

Main Criteria for Exclusion: Not a comprehensive listing but only the key items

Duration of Subject Participation: Provide the actual time for each treatment arm as an average and range for pre-treatment (if relevant), treatment, and post-treatment (if relevant) periods

Duration of Study: Time from commencement of study until completion of analysis

Methods of Evaluation: List primary and secondary efficacy and safety endpoints and briefly describe methods used to measure these using the headings of efficacy, safety, laboratory analyses, and pharmacokinetic parameters.

Pharmacokinetics Results: Brief summary of results for key parameters relevant to this study

Note: The presentations below of the Efficacy Results, Safety Results and Conclusions should not simply repeat descriptions of results or events described elsewhere in the DSUR, but should summarize key outcomes succinctly and clearly identify any new or unexpected findings from the study, comment on their significance, and discuss briefly any potential issues that they raise. Cross references to data tabulated elsewhere in the DSUR are appropriate and preferable to repeating information in this synopsis.

Efficacy Results: The important conclusions concerning efficacy should be concisely described, considering primary and secondary endpoints, pre-specified and alternative statistical approaches and results of exploratory analyses. If efficacy results had an impact on the safety of the patients in the trial or the clinical programme, a more detailed discussion should be given.

Safety Results: Safety results should be presented at three levels. First, the estimate of exposure should lead to a statement about the degree to which the safety can be assessed from the study. Second, there should be reference to any newly identified adverse events or events for which the level of expectedness or concern has changed as a result of this study, and finally, reference to serious adverse events and events of special interest occurring in this study, including death. If the pattern of events is similar to that described in the DCSI, this should be stated; however, more detailed discussion of exceptions should be included.

Conclusion: Provide a brief objective and critical assessment of the results for both safety and efficacy, and if possible a comment on the benefit-risk relationship as perceived from this study. When relevant, the results can be compared to those of other completed, similar studies.

Appendix 6

Comparison of DSUR and PSUR Tables of Contents

The items are listed in the order in which they are expected to appear in the currently required PSUR and for the proposed DSUR. The numbering of the rows is for discussion purposes only. To show that some items are similar or the same even when not in the same order, PSUR entries that generally match those for the DSUR are shown as repeated items in the list, in italics, next to the corresponding DSUR entries.

DSUR	COMPARISON: DSUR vs. PSUR	PSUR
1. Title Page	Same general content	Title Page
2. Table of Contents	Differences as shown herein	Table of Contents
3. Executive Summary	Same general content	Executive Summary
4. Introduction	Same general content	Introduction
5. Worldwide Marketing Authorisation Status	Same general content	Worldwide Market Authorisation Status
6. Update on Actions Taken for Safety Reasons	Same general content	Update of Regulatory Authority or MAH Actions Taken for Safety Reasons
7. Changes to Reference Safety Information	Same general content (DCSI in DSUR, CCSI in PSUR)	Changes to Reference Safety Information
8.	In different location within the DSUR report; for PSUR, mostly estimated market use (under 16. for DSUR)	Patient Exposure
9.	In different location for DSUR. Line listings much more extensive for PSUR; summary tabulations always interval for PSUR (see 12. for DSUR)	Presentation of Individual Case Histories: Line Listings and Summary Tabulations

DSUR	COMPARISON: DSUR vs. PSUR	PSUR
10. Inventory and Status of Ongoing and Completed Interventional Clinical Trials	Much more complete in DSUR for Phase I-III trials. PSUR focus is on special safety studies	Studies: Newly Analysed Company-sponsored studies; Targeted new safety studies planned, initiated or continued during the reporting period; published safety studies
11. Estimated Patient Exposure in Clinical Trials	More extensive estimates for Phase I-IV trials in DSUR. Market use exposure in different DSUR section (see 16.)	*Patient Exposure*
12. Presentation of Safety Data from Clinical Studies (1) Sources of Clinical Study Data (2) General Considerations (3) Line Listings (4) Summary Tabulations	See 9. for PSUR. For DSUR, more background provided concerning data from trials	*Presentation of Individual Case Histories: Line Listings and Summary Tabulations*
13. Significant Findings from Interventional Clinical Trials	Separate section in DSUR. Similar considerations in PSUR (see 9.)	
14. Observational and Epidemiological Studies	Not a separate category in PSUR (see 10.)	
15. Other Information (1) Lack of Efficacy (2) Chemistry, Manufacturing, and Formulation Issues (3) Non-Clinical Findings (4) Literature	Different content in the two reports. Risk Management and Benefit-Risk report information for PSUR found elsewhere in DSUR (see 18.)	Other Information (1) Efficacy-related information (2) Late-breaking information (3) Risk Management programme (4) Benefit-Risk analysis report
16. Information from Marketing Experience	DSUR-specific section for market use data (spontaneous reports, e.g.), but not Phase IV trials (see 13.)	

DSUR	COMPARISON: DSUR vs. PSUR	PSUR
17. Late Breaking Information	See 15. for PSUR.	*Late-breaking information*
18. Overall Safety Evaluation	Similar content	Overall Safety Evaluation
19. Summary of Important Risks	Separate, specific "check list" for DSUR. Covered less formally by inference in PSUR (see 18.)	
20. New Actions Recommended	New section for DSUR	
21. Conclusions	Same general content	Conclusion
22. Appendices to DSUR (1) Inventory of Ongoing and Completed Interventional Clinical Trials (2) DCSI or Safety Sections of IB Available at Beginning of Report Period (3) Line Listing(s) (4) Cumulative Summary Tabulation(s)	Same purpose (all relevant tables and attachments)	Appendix Company Core Data Sheet

Appendix 7

Proposed Table of Contents for a Model Integrated Periodic Safety Report

This Table of Contents is derived directly from the currently required format and content for a PSUR under ICH Guideline E2C. It is enhanced using the proposed format and contents for a DSUR as described in Chapter III of this report and follows the alignment shown in Appendix 6, which compares the current PSUR Table of Contents with that of the newly proposed DSUR. It is presented as a starting point for future discussion and elaboration as a separate project.

For certain items, some annotation is provided (in italics) to indicate some of the details that Working Group VII considered. As is the case for separate DSUR and PSUR documents, this proposal would apply to both commercial and non-commercial investigator-sponsors in those situations when such parties are responsible for both pre- and post-authorisation safety reporting.

Title Page

Table of Contents

Executive Summary

Introduction

Worldwide Marketing Authorisation Status

Update of Regulatory Authority, Trial Sponsor or MAH Actions Taken for Safety Reasons *(actions taken during the reporting period)*

Changes to Reference Safety Information *(DCSI and CCSI when relevant)*

Patient Exposure

- Market Use
- Clinical Trials

Individual Case Histories from Marketing Experience (Excluding Clinical Trials)

- Clinically Significant Individual Case Histories
- Line Listings *(only for special types of reports, such as SUSARs, and by exception)*
- Summary Tabulations *(including spontaneous and solicited reports)*

Clinical Studies

- Inventory and Status of Worldwide Interventional Clinical Trials *(All phases; approved and non-approved indications, dosage forms, populations)*
- Results from Interventional Clinical Trials
  - Completed *(synopsis of results)*
    - Approved Uses
    - Unapproved Uses
  - Ongoing *(synopsis of results if interim analyses conducted during reporting period)*
    - Approved Uses
    - Unapproved Uses
- Line Listings *(only for SUSARs)*
- Summary Tabulations *(All serious adverse events from interventional clinical trials; cumulative)*
- Observational and Epidemiological Studies *(including use of registries)*
  - Completed
  - Ongoing
- Targeted New Safety Studies
  - Completed
  - Ongoing
  - Planned

Other Information

- Efficacy-Related Information
- Chemistry, Manufacturing, and Formulation Issues
- Non-Clinical Findings
- Literature Sources

Late-Breaking Information

Overall Safety Evaluation

- Discussion on:

  Marketed Use Experience

  Investigational Use

Summary of Important Issues *(problem list; update of those previously identified and any new ones)*

- Identified Risks
- Potential Risks
- Important Missing Data *(needed to resolve outstanding issues/risks)*

New Actions Recommended

Conclusions

Appendices

Index

D

E

F

G

H

I

J

L

M

N

S

T

U

W